D0856874

*The County Courts
in Antebellum Kentucky*

ROBERT M. IRELAND

The County Courts in Antebellum Kentucky

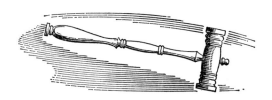

The University Press of Kentucky

ISBN: 0–8131–1257–5

Library of Congress Catalog Card Number: 71–160045

COPYRIGHT © 1972 BY THE UNIVERSITY PRESS OF KENTUCKY

A statewide cooperative scholarly publishing agency serving Berea College, Centre College of Kentucky, Eastern Kentucky University, Kentucky State College, Morehead State University, Murray State University, University of Kentucky, University of Louisville, and Western Kentucky University.

Editorial and Sales Offices: Lexington, Kentucky 40506

Contents

Preface

IT IS PERHAPS IRONIC that some of the most outstanding work in pre-Civil War American historiography concerns national political institutions which touched only lightly the daily lives of most citizens. Still more apparent is the scholarly neglect of the forms of state and county government closest to the people, the institutions which affected their mundane but urgent problems, from business schemes to party patronage to the care of orphans and death settlements. Although a handful of historians have written monographs or essays on the subject of county government, their studies have been essentially digests of duties and powers based upon the dry bones of legislative statutes.[1] Two exceptions to this tendency are Charles S. Sydnor's works on county government in colonial Virginia and the antebellum South and Merle E. Curti's intensive examination of Trempealeau County, Wisconsin, between 1854 and 1880. While both writers do identify basic themes of county constitutional politics, their accounts are nonetheless parts of works much larger in scope and are necessarily brief and somewhat superficial.[2] Aside from Sydnor and Curti, historians of the last two decades have, in large part, left the study of county government to political scientists, whose efforts are usually devoted almost exclusively to analyses of the contemporary scene.[3]

As for Kentucky, studies of the history of her county government are almost nonexistent. They invariably comprise an insubstantial part of larger discussions of current procedures and weaknesses. In some cases these summaries of the historical background of county government are misleading and generally unsatisfactory, and all of them leave much work to be done. The numerous histories of Kentucky's many counties are equally unenlightening with regard to the county courts. Most of them resort to a brief summary of delegated powers and lengthy quotations from court records.

The purpose of this book is to correct partially this historiographical deficiency by identifying the place of the county courts in the constitution and politics of antebellum Kentucky. It seeks not only to define the powers and practices of the county courts but also to establish their relationship with county officials, the legislature, the governor, the higher judicial tribunals, and the towns and cities of the state. An effort is made to estimate the socioeconomic position of the county court justices and to measure the profound impact of two-party politics on the processes of local government. Finally, the study explores the grievances and weaknesses which attached themselves to the county court system, thus revealing why at the mid-nineteenth century it became the object of major constitutional reform.

1 See, for example, Paul W. Wager, *County Government and Administration in North Carolina* (Chapel Hill, N.C., 1928) and Albert Ogden Porter, *County Government in Virginia: A Legislative History, 1607–1904* (New York, 1947).

2 Sydnor, *American Revolutionaries in the Making: Political Practices in Washington's Virginia* (New York, 1965), pp. 74–85, and *The Development of Southern Sectionalism, 1819–1848* (Baton Rouge, La., 1948), pp. 33–53; Curti et al., *The Making of an American Community: A Case Study of Democracy in a Frontier County* (Stanford, Calif., 1959), pp. 259–94.

3 See, for example, Clyde F. Snider, *Local Government in Rural America* (New York, 1957) and Herbert Sydney Duncombe, *County Government in America* (Washington, D.C., 1966).

Acknowledgments

M<small>ANY PEOPLE</small> aided me in the preparation of this book. I am especially grateful to two of my colleagues at the University of Kentucky, to the late Dr. Albert D. Kirwan and to Dr. Steven A. Channing, both of whom read my manuscript in its entirety and offered many valuable suggestions. I am indebted to Professor Jack M. Sosin of the University of Nebraska who as my major advisor contributed immensely to my knowledge of history and my ability to deal with it. I am also grateful to Professor James A. Rawley of the University of Nebraska who served as an inspiring teacher and a helpful counselor. Dr. Jacqueline Bull, head of Special Collections at the University of Kentucky Library, Paul A. Willis, librarian of the University of Kentucky College of Law, and their able associates assisted me in innumerable ways. Also helpful were the late G. Glenn Clift and Miss Joan Brookes-Smith of the Kentucky State Historical Society; James Bentley of the Filson Club; Professor James F. Hopkins, Professor Mary Wilma Hargreaves, and Burton Milward of the Papers of Henry Clay; and Charles L. Atcher, University of Kentucky Archivist. Dr. Thomas D. Clark, formerly of the University of Kentucky, currently Distinguished Professor of History at Indiana University, warmly endorsed my proposal to write on the county courts and enthusiastically supported my project throughout its preparation. I wish to thank the University of Kentucky Research Foundation for providing me with two summer research fellowships and other funds which greatly facilitated the research, writing, and typing of my manuscript. Parts of Chapters 4, 5, and 6 appeared in *The Review of Politics, Mid-America, The Filson Club Quarterly,* and *The American Journal of Legal History,* and I am grateful to the editors of these journals for permitting me to publish this material. The first two maps are reproduced from *Kentucky: A Pictorial History*, edited by J. Winston Coleman, Jr. (Lexington, 1971).

I also extend recognition to my three daughters, Suzanne, Julie, and Betsy, whose ability to tangle up reels of microfilm never ceased to amaze me, and to my wife, Sandra, who on many occasions endured the battles of the county courts, typed several drafts of the manuscript, and contributed in countless other ways to its completion. I thank my wife's parents who, for the past eight summers, have provided a summer retreat for writing and reflection. Above all I am indebted to my mother and father whose support and understanding made my transition from law to history infinitely more enjoyable. It is to them that I dedicate this book.

*The County Courts
in Antebellum Kentucky*

Introduction

THE PRINCIPAL OFFICERS of county government in Kentucky, as throughout colonial America and the antebellum South, were the justices of the peace, and the principal institution, which the magistrates formed collectively, was the county court. This institution as it existed in Kentucky was the end product of centuries of constitutional development, having been most strongly influenced by English tradition. Englishmen invented the county, the commission of peace, and the justices who implemented it. During the late middle ages and throughout the early modern period these local magistrates were empowered individually or in groups to administer the poor laws, supervise the highways, hear petty criminal and civil cases, suppress riots, and generally to perform the business of governing the most significant local unit of the English constitution, the county.[1]

It is not surprising that colonial America adopted much of her local government from her imperial mistress, England. In the colonies of New England and the Middle Atlantic region, county courts, comprising justices of the peace, shared the responsibilities of local control with townships. In the southern colonies the courts completely overshadowed the towns and were the principal agents of the local constitutions. American justices of the peace performed most of the main functions of their English forebears, including the licensing of ferries and taverns and the punishment of vagrants. In most of the colonies the justices of the peace were appointed, usually by the governor, with the advice and consent of his council. In Virginia the magistrates were self-perpetuating, filling vacancies on the county courts themselves.

With independence and maturing, the nature of county government in the new nation gradually changed, especially in New England, the Middle Atlantic states, and the Old West. Here elected boards of county commissioners began to replace justices of the peace and county courts as the nucleus of the county constitution. However, in Kentucky, as in most of the southeastern part of the United States, the county court remained supreme until 1850 or afterward.[2]

As colonial America borrowed from English practice, so Kentucky absorbed much from Virginia in establishing a county governmental structure in 1792. Indeed, in establishing the county courts, the legislature expressly declared in June 1792 that the local tribunals were to continue to have cognizance over all "cases of which the county courts as now constituted have jurisdiction."[3] In jurisdiction and in practice the early county courts of Kentucky differed from their Virginia antecedents in only two matters. The Kentucky courts did not retain vast patronage powers,[4] and the members of the local tribunals, the county court justices, no longer collectively constituted the principal trial courts of the Commonwealth, the courts of quarter sessions.[5] In

1 Sidney Webb Passfield and Beatrice Webb Passfield, *English Local Government: A Series . . . on the Growth and Structure of English Local Government*, 11 vols. (London, 1906), vol. 1, *The Parish and the County*; Bertram Osborne, *Justices of the Peace, 1361–1848* (Shaftesbury, Dorset, 1960); J. H. Gleason, *The Justices of the Peace of England, 1558–1640* (Oxford, 1969).

2 For a brief but useful survey of county government in England, the American colonies, and the United States, see Snider, *Local Government in Rural America*, pp. 3–28.

3 *Acts of Kentucky, 1792*, 1st sess., chap. 35, sec. 4 (hereafter cited as *Acts*).

4 While the first county courts of Kentucky retained the power to appoint constables and the clerk, they lost the power to fill their own vacancies and to name the sheriff, the coroner, the surveyor and the officers of the local militia.

5 In Virginia the justices of the peace met four times a year as the court of quarter sessions and heard civil and criminal cases. The same magistrates thus constituted both the county courts and the courts of quarter sessions. Sydnor, *American Revolutionaries in the Making*, p. 79; Lincoln County

1799 Kentuckians wrote a new Constitution[6] which appreciably enlarged the powers of the county courts over patronage. The new Constitution provided for a "county court . . . in each county" but delegated to the legislature the task of assigning jurisdiction. More important, the document restored to the county courts privileges which had existed before 1792: filling their own vacancies, appointing the sheriff from among their senior members, and selecting the remainder of the county officers.[7] The legislature insured general continuity by allocating practically the same powers and responsibilities as before to the county courts, which remained intact until 1851.

In many ways the county courts were the most vital part of Kentucky government. The Frankfort *Convention* put it this way: "considering the nature of their powers, the number of justices and their location in every county in the

---

Court Order Book, 1791–1794, pp. 3–21 (microfilm, reel M38:2017–18, King Library, University of Kentucky). (Hereafter microfilms of government documents in the King Library will be cited as U.K. microfilms.) The first General Assembly of Kentucky prohibited justices of the peace who constituted the courts of quarter sessions from sitting on the county courts. *Acts, 1792*, 1st sess., chap. 35, sec. 18. In December 1792 the legislature defeated an attempt to merge the two courts and provided that justices of the courts of quarter sessions did not have to perform many of the duties of single justices of the peace; three years later it specified that appointees to that tribunal need not be justices of the peace. *Journal of the House of Representatives of the Commonwealth of Kentucky, 1792*, 2d sess., pp. 67–68 (hereafter cited as *H.J.*); *Acts, 1792*, 2d sess., chap. 2, sec. 1; *Acts, 1795*, chap. 57, sec. 1. Between 1802 and 1804 the legislature abolished the courts of quarter sessions and replaced them with circuit courts, which were staffed by judges who were not justices of the peace. *Acts, 1802*, chap. 1; William Littell, *The Statute Law of Kentucky . . .* , 5 vols. (Frankfort, Ky., 1809–1819), 3:184–86 (hereafter cited as Littell, *Statute Law*).

6 Throughout this study the terms *constitution* and *Constitution* are employed. The term *constitution* refers to the aggregate of the vital parts of government, whereas the term *Constitution* refers expressly to the written, formally adopted charter of the state, the "supreme law" of the Commonwealth.

7 *Constitution of 1799*, Art. 3, secs. 9, 31; Art. 4, secs. 5, 8.

state, the county courts are the most powerful branch of the judiciary, and collectively, capable of exerting a greater influence than all others." Indeed the extent of their authority was such that the courts became, in effect, violations of the separation of powers doctrine. The *Convention* contended that "the anomalous character of its powers, being legislative, executive and judicial, enables this court to wind its way into all the affairs and ramifications of society." W. C. Marshall, delegate to the Constitutional Convention of 1849, remarked that the county court was, of all governmental agencies, closest to the people: "It is a court in which the people of the various counties feel a deep, essential, and . . . abiding interest . . . it is a matter which is brought to their houses and their firesides."[8]

So essential were these local tribunals to Kentuckians that any group of citizens who experienced the slightest inconvenience in reaching the county seat inevitably petitioned the state legislature for the creation of a new county. By 1850 there were one hundred counties in Kentucky, nearly the largest number per square mile and per capita of any state in the Union. So comprehensive and pervasive were the powers and responsibilities of the courts that sooner or later almost everyone in the county, from white adults to slaves, had business with them. County court day attracted many hundreds each month. People brought their deeds to be recorded, their petitions to be heard, and their crops and livestock to be sold after their official business was completed. Court day was also the occasion for politicking and merrymaking, gossiping, and sometimes brawling.

It can even be argued that in states like Kentucky county government as embodied in the county courts was the most

8 Frankfort *Convention*, 27 March, 7 July 1847 (hereafter cited as *Convention*); *Report of the Debates and Proceedings of the Convention for the Revision of the Constitution of the State of Kentucky, 1849* (Frankfort, Ky., 1849), p. 703 (hereafter cited as *Proceedings*).

significant element of the constitution. Most Kentuckians dealt mainly with their county governments, seldom with state agencies, and rarely with national ones. The state government delegated much of its business to the county courts, while national government was relatively inactive, seldom taxing, regulating, protecting, or otherwise aiding Kentuckians.[9] Indeed, one of the federal agencies which most affected people in Kentucky, the Bank of the United States, was more of a private organization than a public one.[10] Thus an examination of the county court system will do much to reveal the lives of antebellum Kentuckians.

[9] Allan Nevins, among others, has argued convincingly that the major loyalties, enterprises, and energies of Americans before the Civil War were locally, not nationally, oriented. "A Major Result of the Civil War," *Civil War History* 5 (September, 1959): 237–50. Throughout most of the old county court system the principal tax imposed by the federal government was a tariff or duty on imports, and it is doubtful that many Kentuckians paid this type of levy. Many in Kentucky doubtless were subject to the federal whiskey tax, but this was a relatively short-lived excise lasting only from 1791 to 1802 and from 1814 to 1817. The type of federal tax which affected most Kentuckians was the "direct tax," but it was imposed only from 1798 to 1801 and from 1814 to 1817. Davis Rich Dewey, *Financial History of the United States* (New York, 1918), pp. 105, 108–11, 120, 138–42, and 277; *Historical Statistics of the United States, 1789–1945* (Washington, D.C., 1952), pp. 297–98. The period under study was also one of little federal aid to, or regulation of, the economy. Carter Goodrich, *Government Promotion of American Canals and Railroads, 1800–1890* (New York, 1960). Furthermore, the principal protective force in antebellum America was not the federal army, which was always small, but rather the state militia, and in Kentucky this institution was especially county-oriented.

[10] For an especially persuasive argument that the nature of the Bank of the United States was more private than public see Harold J. Plous and Gordon E. Baker, "*McCulloch v. Maryland*: Right Principle, Wrong Case," *Stanford Law Review* 9 (July 1957): 710–30.

Chapter I

THE ANATOMY
OF THE COUNTY COURTS

THE JUSTICES of the peace of the counties constituted the membership of the county courts. In addition to serving on the county courts, justices of
the peace individually performed a wide variety of functions including the trial of petty civil and criminal matters,
the taking of depositions, the certifying of legal documents,
and the impaneling of commissions to inspect turnpikes.
Under the first state Constitution, which operated until
1800, the governor selected the magistrates with the advice
and consent of the Senate. Thereafter the courts filled their
own vacancies by recommending two persons to the chief
executive, who was bound to commission one of them
(without approval from the Senate). When new counties
were created from parts of old ones, the members of the
House of Representatives from the old counties in effect
selected the members of the new county court.[1]

Though entitled to fees for their services as individual
magistrates, the justices of the peace received no salaries as
members of the county court. The fact that under the second state Constitution the senior magistrate of each county
was ordinarily commissioned county sheriff was thought to
be reward enough. In some of the more wealthy counties,
however, members of county courts may have received an
illegal income in the form of proceeds from the sale of var-

7

ious county offices. Neither the Constitution nor the laws of the state specified prerequisites for membership on the courts other than that the candidate be a citizen and resident of the state for one year. Legal training was not required. In practice the membership of the county courts was limited to white male adults.

The number of justices of the peace in Kentucky steadily grew throughout the period of the old county court system so that by 1848, on the eve of constitutional change, there were approximately 1,550 magistrates in the state. Most of the impetus for increasing or decreasing the membership of county courts came from the creation of new counties and petitions from county residents. Often when the legislature formed a county it would not only create magistracies for the new county but also decrease the number of magistrates for the now smaller parent county or counties. Residents of counties would frequently petition the legislature for additional justices of the peace in order to secure representation on the county court as well as the benefits of a local magistrate. Sometimes petitioners sought a reduction of court membership, presumably for the sake of economy and efficiency, but the membership of most courts increased steadily until approximately 1830. After that time, although the number of magistrates for the entire state continued to rise, many courts experienced a reduction of membership. Between 1837 and 1844 the membership of forty-four courts increased, while that of thirty courts decreased.

The number of members varied widely from county to county. For example, in 1815 the court of Owen County had seven members and those of Bracken and Grayson had eight, while those of Jefferson and Mercer had twenty-two

1 *Constitution of 1792*, Art. 2, sec. 8; Art. 5, sec. 6; *Constitution of 1799*, Art. 4, secs. 8, 9.

and that of Christian had twenty-seven. Thirty years later the Christian and Jefferson county courts each had twenty-five, and changes had occurred in most counties. Although the legislature never set criteria for determining the number of magistrates in each county, presumably it considered the size of the county, its geographical features, and its population.

Members of the county courts were appointed for life on the condition of good behavior, although few served longer than the time it took to gain the seniority necessary to become sheriff. Some waived that office and continued to serve on the court or sought reappointment as justice of the peace after completing the two-year term of the sheriff. Many left the court voluntarily or involuntarily before becoming eligible for the sheriff's office. Although it is impossible to determine precisely the average length of time justices of the peace spent in office, certain documented speculations can be offered. Basing our guess on the rate of turnover occurring between 1815 and 1820 as evidenced by the entries in the Register of Justices of the Peace for that period, and allowing for the three to four months it usually took to nominate and commission a successor, we estimate the average term of office for a magistrate at approximately eight years. Between 1836 and 1849, based again on the turnover rate as indicated by the Registers for that period, the estimated average term was approximately twelve years. Between 1803 and 1849 approximately 110 men served as magistrates for Fayette County for an average of about eight and a half years. Thirty-seven men were commissioned justice of the peace for the same county between 1792 and 1796, indicating a high rate of turnover and an average term of less than two years. Thus it appears that during the period of the second Constitution the term of a justice of the peace was on the average much longer than it was during the first

Constitution. The fact that after 1799 long service resulted in the sheriffalty doubtless accounts in large part for this development.[2]

The statute enacted by the General Assembly in 1792 establishing the county courts provided that each should meet monthly except during the four months of the year when the courts of quarter sessions convened. Thereafter the legislature from time to time altered the number of meetings the tribunals were to hold each year. Generally the courts of the more populous counties found it necessary to meet every month, while those attracting less business could operate on the schedule established in 1792. A statute of 1821 provided the framework for the remainder of the period of the old county court system: nineteen counties were authorized to hold monthly meetings; the rest were required to hold monthly courts except during those months when the circuit courts convened, usually two or three times a year.[3]

Monday was the day on which all county courts first convened their monthly meetings. The tribunals were required to continue court until all the business of the term was completed, although they did not always do this. Many courts met on the first Monday of the month; others met on the second, third, or fourth Monday. Occasionally the legislature changed the meeting dates of individual courts. Normally certain terms of court were busier than others. The month in which the court of claims was held usually lasted

2 Register of Justices of the Peace, 1815–1820, Isaac Shelby Papers (microfilm, reel 10, Governors' Papers, Kentucky State Historical Society); Register of Justices of the Peace, 1835–1844, Register of Justices of the Peace, 1845–1849 (microfilm, no reel number, Governors' Papers, Kentucky State Historical Society); Fayette County Court Order Books, 1803–1850 (U.K. microfilm, reels M366:1–7). Hereafter microfilms of Governors' Papers, Journals, and Letterbooks in the Kentucky State Historical Society will be cited as G.P.

3 *Acts, 1792*, 1st sess., chap. 35, sec. 4; *Acts, 1821*, chap. 329.

for several days, during which claims of the county were paid and the levy laid for the following year. In Fayette County courts of claims sometimes lasted for as long as eight days and in Bath County one such term extended for a total of twelve days.[4]

While county courts were not circuit courts and were required to hold their sessions at the county seat, William Littell, an early compiler of Kentucky statutes, wrote in 1814 that some tribunals were holding court at unauthorized places. This practice apparently ceased shortly after Littell's published remarks, for not even the ever-critical delegates to the Constitutional Convention of 1849 cited the grievance. Normally when residents of a county found it inconvenient to transact business in the county seat they either petitioned the legislature for the creation of a new county or for a change of the county seat. Both developments were likely to create conflict. A typical instance was the successful effort of the citizens of the Maysville area to have that town named the seat of Mason County, a movement which elicited remonstrances from citizens of the original seat of government, Washington, both before and after the legislatively authorized referendum on the subject.[5]

Routine business of the county courts required a quorum of three. Special business, such as laying the county levy, certifying claims, districting public roads, dispensing patronage, and issuing tavern licenses, required the presence of a majority of the county magistrates. Such matters as claims and the districting of roads were set aside for specific

4 Speech of James W. Nesbitt, *Proceedings*, p. 702. In 1837 the legislature provided that the Jefferson County Court should devote the first week of its monthly meeting to county business and the second week to city affairs, *Acts, 1836–1837*, chap. 410, sec. 2.

5 Littell, *Statute Law*, 4:509; *H.J., 1844–1845*, pp. 184, 219, 254, 279; Remonstrance of Citizens of Mason County, Mason County Historical Society Papers (U.K. microfilm, reel M:120).

months, during which terms all the magistrates were required to attend court or to provide a reasonable cause for absence.[6]

Statistical studies reveal that in some counties many of the magistrates attended all or most of the monthly terms, while in others the justices were far less conscientious. Members of the Fayette County Court during 1841 and 1842, for example, usually attended most of the monthly meetings, whereas those of the Bourbon County Court were less regular. In Fayette fifteen of nineteen justices of the peace who sat on the court throughout the two-year period attended a majority of the tribunal's twenty-four meetings, while in the same period only five of seventeen Bourbon magistrates attended a majority of their court's twenty-two meetings.

A survey of the tax records of four counties for 1792 and of ten counties for 1802, 1830, and 1845 indicates that the general economic level of Kentucky's magistrates was considerably higher than that of the average white adult male.[7] The justices of the peace of Bourbon, Fayette, Lincoln, and Madison counties for 1792 owned nearly nine times as much land, nearly seven times as many slaves, and two and a half times as much other taxable chattel property as the average white male adult of these counties. A decade later magistrates from ten sample counties owned over six and a

---

6 *Acts, 1815–1816*, chap. 385 (claims); William Littell and Jacob Swigert, eds., *A Digest of the Statute Law of Kentucky*, 2 vols. (Frankfort, Ky., 1822), 2:1102 (roads) (hereafter cited as Littell and Swigert, *Digest*).

7 Microfilm of state tax records is located at the Kentucky State Historical Society, Frankfort. The following list is of the counties whose records were examined, with reel numbers in parentheses: Bourbon (27, 29–30), Christian (73, 75), Fayette (100, 102, 104–5), Fleming (111–13), Green (142–43), Henry (172–74), Knox (230–31), Lincoln (243, 245–46), Madison (255–56, 258–59), and Montgomery (292, 294). These counties furnish a balance of geographical location, economy, and population.

half times as much land and over seven times as many slaves as the average white male adult. While in 1830 the ratio of magisterial to white male adult ownership of taxable property declined to slightly less than three to one, by 1845 the margin had increased to nearly three and a half to one.[8] It should be admitted at once that these figures are slightly distorted by the presence on the courts of extremely wealthy persons. Indeed, certain magistrates serving during the earlier sample years may well have been the richest men in their counties. In 1802 Magistrate Green Clay of Madison County owned nearly 40,000 acres of land, making him the largest landowner of the county. In 1794 Clay owned over 100,000 acres of land, over one-fourth the total ownership of all county residents. Likewise, the largest landowner of Knox County in 1803, John Ballinger, who owned over 20,000 acres of land, was a member of the county court. Nevertheless, for magistrates (totaling 536) of all the sample counties in the years examined, over 75 percent owned more taxable property than the average white male adult.

Although Kentucky's many regions varied greatly in wealth and agricultural characteristics, one useful measure of socioeconomic status is slave ownership. A comparison of the slaveholdings of magistrates and white male adults of five counties (Boone, Breckinridge, Butler, Hart, and Mercer) for 1820 reinforces the conclusion that the average county court member of antebellum Kentucky was relatively prosperous. The census of that year indicates that nearly 73 percent of the magistrates of these five counties owned slaves and in a quantity 2.5 times greater than that of nonmagistrate slaveowners. Furthermore, only 33 per-

---

[8] The total tax value of each taxpayer is not given in the tax lists between 1792 and 1803; therefore comparative statistics are based on land, slaves, and livestock, which were the most significant forms of taxable property. Between 1820 and 1845 taxable property also included such miscellaneous chattels as buggies, pianos, and gold watches.

cent of the "heads of families" from these counties owned slaves, making the incidence of ownership among magistrates 2.2 times greater than in the general population. On the average there were 5.6 times more slaves per magistrate than for other heads of families. Of course, wide variations existed among counties, depending in part upon the extent of plantation farming.[9]

The historian is severely limited in any attempt to analyze the occupations of particular social groups prior to 1850. In that year, thanks to the foresight and training of the commercial publisher J. D. B. DeBow, who served as Superintendent of the Federal Census, dependable statistics became available.

The 1850 census reveals that most of the magistrates (80 percent) in ten representative counties were farmers and that very few of them (5.6 percent) were lawyers.[10] Merchants accounted for 4 percent, manufacturers for 2.4 percent, and saddlers and tavern keepers for 1.6 percent each. Rounding out the sample were a bank clerk, a silversmith, a preacher, an auctioneer–newspaper editor, a brick mason, a carpenter, a gunsmith, and a person apparently retired (occupation simply designated "housekeeper"). The average age of the magistrates for the ten counties was 49.2 years. They were slightly older in the more established counties than in the newer ones, the average ages being 51.1 and 46 respectively.

Despite the absence of statistics beyond 1803, it is useful to note that during the early years of the county court system one out of three magistrates was likely to be an officer in the state militia. Data available for all twelve of

9 Kentucky, Population Schedules, Census of 1820 (U.K. microfilm, reels 16–18, 26).

10 The ten counties examined were Fayette, Franklin, Fulton, Garrard, Grant, Larue, Letcher, Ohio, Owsley, and Taylor. Kentucky, Population Schedules, Census of 1850 (U.K. microfilm, vols. 6–7, 12–13, 17).

Kentucky's counties as of June 1792 and for thirty-three of forty-four counties in 1802 and 1803 reveal that nearly one-third of the members of the county courts were militia officers, many holding the rank of captain or higher.[11]

In order to complete the collective portrait of the county court members it should be noted that many justices of the peace were active in state as well as county politics. Between 1792 and 1851 almost a fourth of the members of the lower house and a fifth of the upper house of the legislature were magistrates. Likewise a majority of most of the county magistrates appear to have been active participants in Kentucky's two-party system, which emerged in 1827. Finally, eight of Kentucky's seventeen governors and seven of her twenty-one senators serving during the period of the old county court system had been justices of the peace before their election.[12]

Fayette County provides one of the few surviving examples of extensive contemporary comment on the leaders of county society during the antebellum period, a portrait which furnishes information on the relative prestige of members of a county court. William A. Leavey, a Lexington civic leader and drygoods merchant who was born in 1796, wrote a "Memoir of Lexington" in 1875 that offers reflections on the leading families of Fayette County society throughout much of the life of the old county court system.

[11] Statistics for this analysis were derived from C. Glenn Clift's *"Corn Stalk" Militia of Kentucky, 1792–1811* (Frankfort, Ky., 1957) and from lists of magistrates in the Journal of Governor Isaac Shelby and the Papers of Governor James Garrard, jackets 28–29 (G.P., reels 1, 5).

[12] See Chapters 4 and 6. The governors and the counties in which they served as magistrates were Isaac Shelby (Lincoln), James Garrard (Bourbon), Gabriel Slaughter (Mercer), John Adair (Mercer), Joseph Desha (Mason), Thomas Metcalfe (Nicholas), James Clark (Clark), and John J. Crittenden (Franklin). Adair, Crittenden, and Metcalfe also served in the United States Senate, as did John Edwards (Lincoln), Martin D. Hardin (Franklin), John Pope (Fayette), and George Walker (Jessamine).

If his memoir is accepted as a reliable gauge of the level of prestige of county magistrates, it would seem that members of the court were more respected before 1825 than afterward. Leavey characterizes nearly 30 percent of the magistrates who were appointed between 1792 and 1800 as "respected," "distinguished," "esteemed," or the like. He describes similarly almost half of the magistrates appointed between 1801 and 1825. Yet he depicts only 17 percent of those commissioned after 1825 as leaders of society. Two factors, however, can be cited to impeach Leavey's judgment. First, a majority of the magistrates with whom he probably dealt most directly were appointed after 1825 and familiarity often breeds contempt. Second, the economic level of Fayette County magistrates in 1845 and 1850 was higher than in 1830, and statistics indicate that it rose steadily throughout the last twenty years of the old county court system. Although relatively high economic status does not necessarily guarantee respect from one's peers, such is normally the case. Therefore, with some reservation, it can be concluded that in Fayette County the prestige of county magistrates probably rose between 1792 and 1825 and may have declined thereafter.[13]

In summary the average justice of the peace of Kentucky was close to forty-nine years of age, was most likely to be a farmer, owned substantially more taxable property than the average resident, and received the general, although possibly diminishing, respect of his contemporaries. He was also likely to be a political leader and was often a member of the legislature, an officer in the militia, or both. During the first decade of the old county court system he was likely to

[13] William A. Leavey, "A Memoir of Lexington and Its Vicinity with Some Notice of Many Prominent Citizens and Its Institutions of Education and Religion," *Register, Kentucky State Historical Society* 40 (1941): 107–31, 253–67, 353–75; 41 (1942): 44–62, 107–37, 250–60, 310–46; 42 (1943): 26–53; Fayette County Tax Records, 1830, 1850 (microfilm copy, reels 102, 105).

serve as a magistrate for approximately two years, while in the remaining decades, influenced by the prospect of the sheriffalty, he usually held office for a much longer period of time. Thus the majority of the magistrates possessed the potential for dynamic leadership in county government. Whether they utilized that potential is another matter.

Chapter 2

THE JUDICIAL BUSINESS
OF THE COUNTY COURTS

THE BUSINESS of the county courts was substantial, encompassing executive, legislative, and judicial functions. The most significant and sometimes controversial elements of the jurisdiction of the courts were wills and estates, the poor and the vagrant, guardians and apprentices, ferries, milldams, bastardy, emancipation, Negro felonies, the fining of officers, appeals from magistrates, roads, taxes, appropriations, towns, and patronage. The last five concerns will be treated in other chapters. The remainder of this important business, most of which was judicial in nature, will be discussed here.

A survey of county court order books indicates that most of the judicial business of the courts involved probating wills and overseeing the administration of estates.[1] This grant of jurisdiction also encompassed the certification of executors, the appointment of administrators, and the selection of commissioners to appraise the estate, settle the accounts of the executor or administrator, and divide the property, including any rights of dower.[2]

Conflicts sometimes arose in probating estates, both between county courts and between county and circuit courts. The court of the county in which the decedent resided had jurisdiction over his estate, and normally there was no problem identifying the proper tribunal. Occasionally, though, disputes between county courts occurred, especially when the decedent possessed several farms, as in the case of James Speed, who owned property in both Garrard and Scott counties. Both county courts attempted to exercise jurisdiction over Speed's estate, and ultimately the Court of Appeals had to resolve the dispute, ruling that the Scott County Court had jurisdiction over the matter since it had heard the case first.[3]

Circuit courts intervened more frequently into the probate affairs of county courts than did other county courts. As the principal repositories of equity jurisdiction in the judicial system of the state, circuit courts were empowered to hear bills in equity contesting wills and attacking the final accountings of county courts with executors and administrators. One critic proclaimed that practically every case in probate ultimately ended up before a circuit court in equity.[4] Suits contesting wills were infrequent but sometimes resulted in decrees overturning the orders of county courts. For example, the heirs of Jeconias Singleton successfully attacked his will, which had been validated by the Woodford County Court, on the grounds that it was a product of insanity and undue influence.[5]

[1] Over two-thirds of the orders entered in the Fayette County Court Order Book for 1845 concerned wills and estates. More than half of the orders of 1816 pertained to the same subject. In Bracken County approximately 40 percent of the court's orders for the same sample years involved probate matters. Fayette County Court Order Book, 1811–1817, pp. 357–491 (U.K. microfilm, reel M366:2); Fayette County Court Order Book, 1840–1846, pp. 439–534 (U.K. microfilm, reel M366:6); Bracken County Court Order Book, 1797–1817, pp. 421–47 (U.K. microfilm, reel M478:120); Bracken County Court Order Book, 1835–1845, pp. 427–72 (U.K. microfilm, reel M478:121).

[2] Acts, 1796–1797, pp. 163–71.

[3] Pawling v. Speed's Executor, 5 T. B. Monroe 580 (1827).

[4] Frankfort Kentucky Yeoman, 17 December 1846 (hereafter cited as Yeoman).

[5] In re Singleton's Will, 8 Dana 315 (1839). The decisions of circuit courts were not printed. The decision reported is that of the Court of Appeals,

More frequently parties sought bills in equity to transfer the process of final accounting with executors or administrators from the county to the circuit court. The Court of Appeals ruled that whichever court initiated final accounting should retain the action to its completion.[6] However, in the case of a county court its decree was thereafter subject to review by a circuit court sitting in equity. Thus in the case of *Kellar's Executors* v. *Beelor* the Jefferson County Circuit Court partially revised a final accounting of the Jefferson County Court, while in *Saunders' Heirs* v. *Saunders' Executors* a circuit court obtained complete jurisdiction over the final accounting process to the exclusion of a county court since the executors had waited to apply to the latter tribunal for the appointment of commissioners to settle their accounts only after the commencement of a suit in chancery.[7]

It was natural that the state should entrust the county courts with the duty of appointing guardians and masters and protecting orphans and apprentices since it delegated to them the analogous responsibility of supervising executors and estates. The antebellum period of Kentucky history was an era of cholera epidemics, smallpox outbreaks, and relatively high mortality rates, all of which created a substantial orphan population. In the event of the death of both parents the county court interceded, appointing a suitable person guardian of the minor children, taking bond from him as security, and requiring the appointee to

---

to which tribunal the ruling of the circuit court was appealed. Nonetheless this report indicates the role of the circuit court in the litigation, as do all the relevant cases cited.

6 *Saunders' Heirs* v. *Saunders' Executors*, 2 Littell 314 (1822).

7 *Kellar's Executors* v. *Beelor*, 5 T. B. Monroe 573 (1827); *Saunders' Heirs* v. *Saunders' Executors*, 2 Littell 314 (1822). The report of the latter case does not indicate which county was involved.

file an inventory of the estate and to make periodic accountings of receipts and expenditures.[8]

In their efforts to see that estates of orphans were not wasted away, county courts sometimes found it necessary to remove guardians and replace them with others deemed more competent. The Court of Appeals greatly facilitated this process by ruling in 1812, in the case of *Piat* v. *Allaway*, that it had no right to review the act of removing a guardian since the proceeding was exclusively executive, not judicial.[9] It was not until 1835, rather late in the period of the old county court system, that this decision was reversed in the case of *Isaacs* v. *Taylor*. The facts of this controversy clearly compelled a rejection of the earlier decision. The Marion County Court appointed Nancy Isaacs guardian for her infant son and then removed her without notice, appointing in her stead the executor of her husband's estate. The high court was obviously appalled at this action, which removed the "natural guardian" in favor of the executor, "the last competent person on earth who should be the guardian." While paying superficial respect to *Piat* v. *Allaway*, the high court in effect overruled it and remanded the case to the county court, requiring it to give Mrs. Isaacs notice and to show cause for her removal.[10]

Although until 1835 the county courts were relatively immune from judicial review of their orders removing guardians, they were not free from the supervision of equity in other matters affecting these officials. To straighten out accounts and fees, beleaguered guardians and ex-guardians frequently sought the services of the local circuit judge sitting as a chancellor in equity. Indeed the justices themselves utilized the services of the circuit courts to compel

---

[8] For the basic statute regarding guardians see *Acts, 1796–1797*, pp. 145–48.

[9] 2 Bibb 544 (1812).

[10] 3 Dana 600 (1835).

errant guardians to restore wasted assets to the estates of orphans.[11]

County courts were required by statute to bind out as apprentices all orphans "who hath no estate, or not sufficient for maintenance out of the profits."[12] Guardians could bind out orphans with adequate assets "to such persons for learning an art or trade" with the approval of the county court.[13] These provisions, along with those requiring the magistrates to bind out illegitimate children and all progeny of white and free black parents who were too poor to maintain them, meant that a substantial portion of the judicial business of the county courts concerned masters and apprentices. Most of this business was routine—hearing proof by fellow justices or other county officials that a particular family was too impoverished to maintain their children, ordering infants bound out, securing bond from newly appointed masters, and ordering apprentices bound to new masters when old ones died or resigned. Occasionally friends of apprentices, or the apprentices themselves, appeared under a provision of the law requiring the courts to hear their complaints of maltreatment from masters. Such proceedings often resulted in fines being imposed upon masters and, in some cases, in their removal.

The decisions of county courts concerning masters and apprentices were also subject to higher judicial revision. Aggrieved apprentices or their friends or parents could appeal to the Court of Appeals decisions of county courts binding them out. In *Robarts* v. *Desforges* the high tribunal reversed an order binding out the son of James Robarts since the record did not show that the father had been properly summoned before the court at the time of the

[11] *Mason County Justices* v. *Bridges*, Mercer County Circuit Court Judgments, September 1808 (U.K. microfilm, reel M310:2108–9).

[12] *Acts, 1796–1797*, sec. 2, p. 147.

[13] Ibid., sec. 3, p. 148.

original proceeding.[14] The same rights extended to Negro children. In *Payne* v. *Long* and *Rachel* v. *Emerson* the high tribunal reversed county court orders binding out Negro children on the grounds that the persons with whom they had been staying had not been notified of the impending proceedings.[15]

Although there is no evidence of direct criticism, it is apparent that many county courts were less than efficient in the performance of their responsibilities as executors of the state's guardianship and apprenticeship statutes. In 1835 the Senate considered a bill which suggested that the local tribunals failed to address themselves promptly to the needs of orphans and apprentices. The bill provided, among other things, that the county courts should "always [be] open for . . . appointing guardians and binding out apprentices."[16] The Senate defeated the proposal, and the grievances of orphans and apprentices were aired no more in public even at the hypercritical Constitutional Convention of 1849. Yet the causes of the complaints which produced the bill of 1835 probably persisted.

The county courts administered the poor laws throughout the period of the old county court system and administered the vagrancy laws until 1839, when this authority was transferred to the circuit courts. The tribunals were required to provide for the poor out of the county levy and to bind or hire out vagrants, depending on whether they were minors or not. A person was "poor" if he was "incapable of procuring a livelihood" because of some "personal debility or otherwise"; he was a "vagrant" if he was an "able bodied person" who was a "beggar," a wife-deserter,

---

14 2 A. K. Marshall 39 (1819).

15 Ibid., p. 158 (1819); 6 B. Monroe 280 (1845).

16 *Journal of the Senate of the Commonwealth of Kentucky, 1834–1835*, p. 326 (hereafter cited as *S.J.*).

or an "idle . . . and dissolute person, rambling about without any reasonable means of subsistence." [17] In order to classify a person as a vagrant the county courts had to proceed judicially and try him before a jury.

The paucity of officially reported vagrancy cases before the Court of Appeals suggests that few people convicted by the county courts under the vagrancy laws appealed their decisions. [18] The fact that the right of appeal was not expressly given in the statutes and the impoverished condition of the defendants no doubt largely explain the almost total absence of judicial review.

The only apparent controversy over the poor laws arose from the tendency of certain impoverished heads of families to send their charges into other counties to attach themselves to the county dole. The legislature outlawed such activity in 1798. [19]

Although the legislature authorized county courts to administer aid to the poor by means of overseers, a system which had been used in colonial Virginia as well as England, most courts appear simply to have assigned to each poor person a responsible citizen of the community through whom funds were channeled. In some instances, especially in the case of infants, the persons in charge of the poor appear to have taken them into their homes.

Poor relief became more institutionalized beginning in 1821, when the legislature authorized the county courts to build poorhouses and most of them did, apparently agree-

[17] *Acts, 1793*, chap. 38, sec. 2; *Acts, 1795*, chap. 55, sec. 1.

[18] The reports of the Court of Appeals contain only two cases concerning vagrancy, *Gatliff* v. *Commonwealth*, 5 Littell 166 (1824), and *Frishe* v. *Commonwealth*, 6 Dana 318 (1838). The first case did not involve the vagrant but the person who hired him, and the second was appealed from the City Court of Louisville, which had jurisdiction over vagrancy cases within the city limits.

[19] Littell, *Statute Law*, 2:87.

ing with the Fayette County magistrates that such structures would more "economically maintain" the impoverished.[20] The statute also authorized courts to appoint a single "keeper" or "superintendent" to manage each poorhouse and several (usually three) "overseers" or "managers" to supervise the "keeper." After construction of a poorhouse a court allocated a lump sum to the superintendent for care of the poor and only rarely made appropriations to individual paupers as had been done under the old system.

In 1796 the General Assembly authorized county courts to "establish public ferries across those rivers or creeks within their respective counties, whenever they shall deem it necessary," to take performance bonds from owners, to set rates, and to discontinue franchises because of disuse.[21] Since ferries were usually profitable ventures and were vital to transportation in an era when bridge construction was rather crude, private entrepreneurs as well as towns and cities eagerly sought franchises to build and operate them. Competition for these franchises created conflicts and litigation. Aggrieved parties could appeal county court decisions to the Court of Appeals according to an express provision in the act of 1796.[22] Many of the battles involved private entrepreneurs contesting the claims of towns and cities to ferry rights across the Ohio River. Before 1806 the legislature had reserved the right to grant franchises on the Ohio. Yet so many county courts awarded franchises for Ohio River traffic that in 1806 the General Assembly had to pass a statute confirming the validity of those grants and authorizing the county courts henceforth to award such

[20] *Acts, 1821*, chap. 309; Fayette County Court Order Book, 1821–1824, p. 81 (U.K. microfilm, reel M366:3).

[21] *Acts, 1796–1797*, pp. 41–43.

[22] Ibid., sec. 3, p. 42.

franchises. Subsequently the Court of Appeals ruled that the courts could grant franchises only to owners of land on the river.[23] Certain towns, claiming ownership of all their shoreline, sought to take advantage of this decision by obtaining franchises to the exclusion of private parties already established in business.

One of the most bitterly contested fights concerned the efforts of the town of Maysville to secure the exclusive right to a ferry franchise across the Ohio River. The Mason County Court had made five different grants before the town applied for a franchise in September 1827. Summonses were issued to all five ferry owners, three of whom appeared with their attorneys at the October term of the court and successfully opposed the town's efforts to secure a franchise. The town appealed to the Court of Appeals and not only secured a right to have a franchise established in its name but in effect eliminated the other five franchises, two because of disuse and three because they did not own the land adjacent to the river as required by the high tribunal.[24]

Similar battles ensued in Campbell County between private entrepreneurs and the towns of Newport and Covington. In Newport the fracas was particularly bitter. In 1795 the Campbell County Court awarded James Taylor the right to operate a ferry between Newport and Cincinnati. Taylor operated the ferry without contest until 1830, when the town of Newport petitioned the county court for the exclusive right to the franchise on the grounds that it, not Taylor, owned the land adjacent to the river where the enterprise was headquartered. This challenge touched off a controversy which lasted for twenty years and involved

---

23 *Trustees of Jefferson Seminary* v. *Wagnon*, 2 A. K. Marshall 379 (1820).

24 *Trustees of Maysville* v. *Boon*, 2 J. J. Marshall 224 (1829); Martin Brown to John L. Langhorne, 9 October 1829, Mason County Historical Papers (U.K. microfilm, reel M120).

two legal battles and a political struggle within the county court. The matter was finally resolved in 1850 when the Court of Appeals once and for all confirmed the validity of Taylor's franchise.[25]

The town of Covington fared better than its neighbor, Newport, when in 1830 it successfully obtained a franchise from the Campbell County Court to the exclusion of Samuel Kennedy, who had operated a ferry on the shoreline of the town for many years. The principal question in the case was whether Kennedy owned the land upon which the ferry was established. On appeal to the Court of Appeals he sought to introduce new evidence proving his title, but his appeal was denied, eliciting a vigorous dissenting opinion from Chief Justice Robertson and leaving Covington as the only ferry operator within town limits.[26]

The county courts of Kentucky derived their authority over milldams from earlier laws enacted by the legislature of Virginia. In 1797 the General Assembly of Kentucky codified these laws into one statute which was the basic source of jurisdiction over milldams for the rest of the period of the old county court system.[27] Milldams, crucial to the economic existence of essentially agricultural Kentucky, formed an integral part of grist mills upon which farmers and millers depended. Practically every major farm had its own. In order to build one, a prospective miller had to go through a rather elaborate judicial procedure in the court of the county in which the dam was to be located.

[25] *Trustees of Newport* v. *Taylor*, 6 J. J. Marshall 134 (1831); *City of Newport* v. *Taylor's Heirs*, 11 B. Monroe 361 (1850). For the relation of the ferry dispute to county court politics see L. H. Rugg et al. to Governor William Owsley, 15 December 1847, Owsley Papers, jacket 705 (G.P., reel 98).

[26] *Kennedy* v. *Trustees of Covington*, 4 J. J. Marshall 538 (1830).

[27] *Acts, 1796–1797*, pp. 196–99.

The crucial question, regardless of whether the applicant owned all or part of the lands surrounding the watercourse upon which he desired to construct his milldam, was whether the operation would damage the "mansion houses, offices, curtelages, gardens, or orchards" of his neighbors or menace the wildlife, fish, and health of the area.[28] The court ordered the sheriff to summon a jury of twelve to conduct an investigation. If this jury found that the proposed dam would cause damages or constitute a menace to health, the court refused to authorize it. However, the power of the county courts over milldams was not absolute. The legislature periodically withdrew major streams and rivers from the jurisdiction of the county courts. For example, in January of 1817 the General Assembly forbade county courts to permit further milldam construction "over the Beech and Rolling Forks of Salt River." Yet one year later it passed a special law empowering the Washington County Court to authorize Edward Berry and Philips Mattingly to build a milldam upon the Beech Fork under proper supervision.[29]

Furthermore, as with ferries, parties could appeal county court orders on milldams to the Court of Appeals, which was empowered virtually to retry such cases. Thus the Court of Appeals decided in 1844 in the case of *Trabue* v. *Macklin* to remand an order from the Franklin County Court authorizing Macklin to build a dam nine feet high on the grounds that the proposed structure was too high. In *Eubank* v. *Pence*, decided in 1824, the high court reversed an order of the Shelby County Court permitting dam construction on the grounds that the local tribunal had failed to ascertain whether "fish of passage will in any degree be obstructed," while in *Wootten* v. *Campbell*, decided in 1838, the court reversed an order of the Spencer County Court on the grounds that the health of the neighborhood

28 Ibid., sec. 3, p. 196.
29 *Acts, 1816–1817*, chap. 18; *Acts, 1817–1818*, chap. 163.

would be threatened by the proposed dam of Robert S. Campbell.[30]

As the chief judicial vehicles for dealing with the parents of illegitimate children, the county courts rendered judgments on charges of bastardy against men brought by single women. Normally a man found guilty was charged a sum of money judged necessary by the court to maintain the child during its infancy. If the father could furnish bond securing this money, which was usually payable over a period of years, he was released from the custody of the court; if not, he was jailed until he rendered oath as a debtor.[31]

The proceedings of county courts in matters of bastardy were subject to judicial review by the Court of Appeals, but review was not as frequent as in other types of cases, such as those dealing with ferries. The high tribunal ruled that the county courts had wide discretion in assessing judgments for maintenance, upheld the right of the county courts to punish white fathers of mulatto children (provided that the mother was a free Negro), and ruled that there should be no appeal from judgments of acquittal. However, it did prevent county courts from hearing charges against fathers who resided out of the county or who committed their alleged deeds out of the state and decreed that circuit courts had concurrent jurisdiction over suits to enforce maintenance judgments.[32]

County courts presided over the emancipation of slaves. Slaveholders could free slaves by one of two methods: a

---

[30] 4 B. Monroe 407 (1844); 5 Littell 338 (1824); 7 Dana 204 (1838).

[31] *Acts, 1795,* chap. 11.

[32] *Evarts* v. *Commonwealth,* 2 B. Monroe 55 (1841); *Williams* v. *Blincoe,* 5 Littell 171 (1824); *Commonwealth* v. *Sandford,* 5 Littell 289 (1824); *Carter* v. *Kilburn,* 1 A. K. Marshall 463 (1819); *Tanner* v. *Allen,* Littell's Selected Cases 25 (1806); *Hamilton* v. *Commonwealth,* 3 T. B. Monroe 212 (1826).

document executed before the court or a provision in a will. Courts recorded the means of emancipation, issued decrees of freedom to the former slaves, and, if necessary, required the former owner or his executor to post bond to insure that the former slaves did not become charges against the county.[33] Sometimes a testator sought to circumvent this contingency by providing in his will that the slaves had to post bond in order to secure freedom.[34]

Such decrees were subject to review in the circuit courts. This happened most often after the emancipator had died. Executors or heirs sometimes challenged the validity of emancipation in a proceeding at equity in the appropriate circuit court.[35] In some cases the slaves themselves brought suit in the circuit court to secure freedom under an instrument or deed. For example, in *Hill* v. *Squire* slaves of a recently deceased slaveowner successfully sued the executor in the Madison County Circuit Court to require him to free them under a provision of the will.[36]

The local tribunals were also empowered to try cases originating under an act passed in 1808 preventing free Negroes from emigrating into the state and to hear all prosecutions against allegedly felonious slaves. The Court of Appeals significantly altered the first grant of jurisdiction when in 1832 it reversed a conviction of the Knox County Court on the grounds that the act unconstitutionally denied the defendant a trial by jury.[37] Prosecutions against slaves for alleged felonies were transferred to the circuit courts in 1819.[38]

[33] Littell, *Statute Law,* 2:119–20.

[34] See, for example, the case of *Hill* v. *Squire*, 12 B. Monroe 557 (1851).

[35] See, for example, *Johnson's Administrator* v. *Johnson's Heirs*, 8 B. Monroe 470 (1848).

[36] 12 B. Monroe 557 (1851).

[37] *Doram and Ryan* v. *Commonwealth*, 1 Dana 331 (1832).

[38] *Acts, 1808–1809*, chap. 78, sec. 7; Littell and Swigert, *Digest*, 1:371, 2:1149–64.

Fining county officers for neglecting their duties and entertaining suits against them for damages resulting from misfeasance comprised part of the jurisdiction of the county courts. More often than not courts threatened rather than fined either their own members or other county officials for alleged neglect of duty. For example, at its April term of 1835, the Fayette County Court summoned Sheriff Asa Thomson to show cause why he should not be fined "for failing to give the necessary attention to this court as required by law" and at the same term heard Thomson's explanation and released him from the order.[39] Yet on occasion the courts did fine officials, as in 1817 when the Greenup County Court fined George W. Davis, deputy sheriff of the county, for failing to return his list of fines collected in 1816 within the prescribed period of time.[40] County courts also heard actions by sheriffs against their deputies for damages resulting from alleged delinquencies in office and actions brought by paymasters of the militia against sheriffs for failure to collect and return militia fines.[41]

The county courts possessed limited appellate jurisdiction, the most significant part of which involved appeals from decisions of individual justices of the peace. Originally the county tribunals heard appeals from magistrates' courts when the judgments involved twenty-five shillings or more. In 1812 the legislature raised the limitation on the jurisdiction of magistrates from five pounds to fifty dollars, provided that the county courts retain their appellate powers over judgments ranging from twenty-five shillings to five

39 Fayette County Court Order Book, 1833–1836, pp. 260, 267 (U.K. microfilm, reel M366:5).

40 Gabriel Slaughter Papers, jacket 175 (G.P., reel 20).

41 See, for example, *Dye et al.* v. *Knox*, 1 Bibb 573 (1809) and *Poague* v. *Culver*, 5 Littell 132 (1824).

pounds, and gave the circuit courts the right to hear appeals from judgments in excess of five pounds.[42]

It is not known whether any magistrates ever decided appeals from their own judgments as members of the county court, although the practice was never proscribed by the legislature or the Court of Appeals. The order books do not shed light on the question since the names of justices of the peace whose decisions were appealed were never recorded. The fact that critics of the old county court system never cited the problem is evidence against the existence of self-review but does not eliminate the possibility altogether. Whether or not members of county courts reviewed their own judgments, it is clear that the magistrates in general were not reluctant to reverse decisions of their brethren. For example, in 1816 the Fayette County Court heard twenty-four appeals, affirmed ten decisions, dismissed nine (usually for want of prosecution), and reversed five. In the same year the Bracken County Court heard three appeals and reversed two decisions.[43]

If the ability of magistrates to hear appeals from their own decisions did not trouble critics of the old county court system, inconsistency of the appellate review did. Larkin J. Proctor, delegate from Lewis County to the Constitutional Convention of 1849, accused the court of his county of inconsistency in two rulings on the question of whether an appeal could be heard from a magistrate's judgment of less than twenty-five shillings when the amount of the claim had exceeded that amount.[44] It was entirely possible for inconsistencies to occur since membership on County Courts hearing appeals was not always the same and the appellate

[42] *Acts, 1796–1797*, sec. 8, p. 16; *Acts, 1811–1812*, chap. 342, secs. 1, 4.

[43] Fayette County Court Order Book, 1811–1817, pp. 358–491 (U.K. microfilm, reel M366:2); Bracken County Court Order Book, 1797–1817, pp. 421–47 (U.K. microfilm, reel 478:120).

[44] *Proceedings*, pp. 698–99.

decisions of the courts were not subject to review by a higher tribunal.

As the first half of the nineteenth century progressed and the amount of litigation, including that before magistrates, increased, the number of appeals from justices of the peace to county courts decreased. No direct evidence explaining the diminution is available, but it can be speculated that the governor may have taken over some of the appeals in his capacity as a legal officer with powers of remission and pardon.

The first and second Constitutions of Kentucky vested broad power with the governor to remit fines imposed by judicial tribunals.[45] The chief executives of the state rarely invoked the power of remission before 1808 but thereafter increasingly remitted fines imposed by lower courts. In his two years as governor from 1832 to 1834, John Breathitt remitted more fines—363—than any other chief executive during the period of the old county court system. Thereafter the number of remissions, although still substantial, declined slightly and then leveled off.[46]

In remitting fines the governors often acted as competitors of the county courts since many of the appeals to the chief executive were from justices of the peace and might instead have gone to the local tribunals. Less often did the governors serve as sources of appeal from decisions of the county courts themselves, probably because most of them followed a ruling of the attorney general issued in 1804 in which he argued that the chief executive could remit only fines "accruing to the benefit of the state, not to the county, any corporation or any individual."[47] Since most fines im-

---

[45] *Constitution of 1792*, Art. 2, sec. 10; *Constitution of 1799*, Art. 3, sec. 11.

[46] The above statistics were obtained from the journals of the governors (G.P., reels 1, 2, 4, 6, 8, 10, 11, 24, 27, 34, 36, 45, 53–55, 109).

[47] Christopher Greenup Journal, p. 6 (G.P., reel 8).

posed by the county courts "accrued to the benefit of the county," strict observance of this ruling would have limited severely the right of governors to remit fines imposed by local tribunals. The great majority of fines remitted by governors were those imposed for failure to file lists of taxable property since such fines accrued to the benefit of the state, but not all governors followed the ruling of 1804. For example, in 1817 Governor Gabriel Slaughter remitted a fine imposed against Herbert G. Waggener, a justice of the peace for Adair County, for missing claims court even though the penalty accrued to the benefit of the county.[48]

The county courts played a vital role in the judicial system of the state. Their jurisdiction encompassed many different questions, requiring their members to be familiar with the laws governing wills and estates, ferries, roads, guardians and orphans, apprentices, bastards, milldams, and numerous other specialties. In the words of Squire Turner, a lawyer from Madison County and a delegate to the Constitutional Convention of 1849, a knowledge of so many technical areas of the law "require[d] a good deal of study and reflection."[49]

Yet where they were not subject to judicial or administrative review, as in the case of appeals from single magistrates, the courts were guilty of inconsistent adjudication. This situation deepened the disaffection in which they were held by their constituents and led ultimately to constitutional review and revision.

---

[48] Slaughter Papers, jacket 176 (G.P., reel 20).
[49] *Proceedings,* p. 700.

Chapter 3

THE FINANCIAL BUSINESS OF THE COUNTY COURTS

M UCH OF the business of the county courts concerned matters of taxation and appropriations, roads, and other internal improvements. While some phases of this business were judicial, most were either executive or legislative. Both the extent of the county courts' authority in these cases, usually involving substantial delegations of power from the legislature, and the controversies they aroused require special consideration.

The county courts played an important part in the assessment and collection of state taxes. From the beginning of statehood they were empowered to lay the counties off into tax districts, to appoint tax commissioners for each district who were to take lists of taxable property from local residents and assess the property, and to name a collector, usually the sheriff. The collector, relying on the assessment of the commissioners, collected the taxes and turned them over to the state treasury.[1] Although critics and reformers from time to time attacked this procedure, it remained basically intact throughout the period of the old county court system.

While the state tax system operated efficiently for the most part, the performance and pay of the court-appointed tax commissioners sparked some controversy. The first revenue act of Kentucky specified that the commissioners should be paid six shillings a day for their services, a rate which the legislature altered periodically so that by 1837 commissioners were receiving a maximum of $1.50 for each day's work.[2] During much of the period of the old county court system the General Assembly granted the county courts some discretion in setting the commissioners' pay, although occasionally a dispute arose over how much a commissioner was entitled to receive. Pay schedules were especially prone to controversy when courts tried to circumvent *per diem* statutory rates by contracting in advance with a commissioner to take in lists for a lump sum regardless of the number of days spent on the job. Such was the case in Warren County in January 1809 when the county court contracted with Enas Daniel to act as a tax commissioner for $66, even though the revenue statute provided that the commissioners should be paid $1 a day for their services. Either the court knew what it was about or Daniel was dishonest, for in October, ignoring his contract, he presented the magistrates with a bill for $144, claiming he had spent 144 days taking in lists of taxable property in his district. The county court rejected his claim and awarded him $66 according to the terms of the contract, a decision which was upheld by the Court of Appeals on the grounds that a county court had absolute jurisdiction over the question of how much tax commissioners should be paid.[3]

In 1842 this question presented itself in a much more comprehensive form directly connected to the question of the commissioners' competence. The latter issue, which had been simmering for some time, involved the merits of con-

---

1 See *Acts, 1792,* 1st sess., chap. 6, which established the basic system of assessing and collecting state taxes throughout the period of the old county court system.

2 Ibid., sec. 6; *Acts, 1836–1837,* chap. 399, sec. 4.

3 *County Court of Warren* v. *Daniel,* 2 Bibb 573 (1812).

tinuing to allow the county courts the power to appoint the commissioners. For instance, in August 1834 the Fayette County Court ordered several persons to examine and correct many errors in the assessment books of the tax commissioners.[4] Such incidents grew more and more common so that by November 1839 Governor Charles Wickliffe in his annual message to the legislature had ample reason to deliver a blast at the performance of the commissioners. Wickliffe contended that "persons wholly incompetent [were] often selected by the county courts for reasons other than their fitness for the station." The governor also criticized the latest revenue statute, which gave certain latitude to the county courts in establishing the pay for the commissioners. He argued that this system gave rise to favoritism and inequality in allotting pay and submitted that the cost of taking in lists of taxable property in Scott County exceeded that of Shelby County by 20 percent, while the total revenue obtained from the former was nearly 40 percent less than that from the latter. He recommended that the legislature take away from the county courts the power of appointing tax commissioners and transfer it to the governor, who would appoint one county tax assessor responsible for selecting his own deputies.[5]

Wickliffe's indictment of the commissioners did result in certain reforms, but not of the kind he had suggested. Instead of divesting the county courts of some of their patronage and creating a new officer, the legislature retained the old system and imposed requirements designed to make the commissioners' lists more reliable. In 1840 it passed a law requiring the county clerk to audit more carefully the commissioners' books, and in 1842 it lowered the commissioners' pay and imposed penalties for errors in their re-

---

[4] Fayette County Court Order Book, 1833–1836, p. 87 (U.K. microfilm, reel M366:5).

[5] H.J., 1839–1840, pp. 16–17.

turns. The latter measure compounded the problem rather
than solved it. Less pay produced even less competent commissioners as well as protests from certain county courts
which found the task of appointing acceptable officers even
more onerous. Property valuations for 1843 declined substantially, and many blamed this on the newer and more
inept class of commissioners. Some commentators recommended transferring the power of appointing commissioners from the county courts to either the circuit courts or the
governor. The legislature did neither, nor did it raise the
pay of the commissioners; instead it simply tightened once
more the requirements of auditing, and the crisis apparently abated since nothing further was heard on the matter.[6]

There were other shortcomings in the county courts' administration of the revenue laws. Occasionally the justices
of the peace would appoint minors, constables, or themselves as tax commissioners—or even no one at all. This gave
rise to remedial legislation forbidding the appointment of
minors, magistrates, or constables and empowering the state
auditor to appoint commissioners if a court failed to do so.
It was found that in the smaller counties it was necessary to
appoint constables to take in lists, so the prohibition against
constables was removed two years after its imposition.[7]

The legislature also assigned to the county courts the responsibility of adjusting lists of taxable property and imposing fines on those who failed to cooperate with the tax
commissioners. Accordingly, the courts not infrequently
corrected excessive assessments by commissioners. For example, at its August court in 1834 the Fayette County Court
ordered that J. Logan "be released from the payment of
taxes on $2,000 worth of taxable property charged by the

[6] *Acts, 1839–1840*, chap. 39; *Acts, 1841–1842*, chap. 428; Frankfort *Commonwealth,* 7 November, 5 December 1843 (hereafter cited as *Commonwealth*); *Acts, 1844–1845*, chap. 84.

[7] *Acts, 1839–1840*, chap. 355; *Acts, 1841–1842*, chap. 15; *Acts, 1843–1844*,
chap. 183, sec. 2; chap. 230.

commissioner of tax for the present year more than he had."[8]

The problem of fining those who failed to turn in tax lists normally occupied more of the court's time. Over fifty such cases were docketed in the Fayette County Court Order Book during the June term of 1838. In one rather celebrated case the Court of Appeals ruled in the same year that the Fayette County Court could not require Madison C. Johnson, a prominent lawyer who was being prosecuted for failure to turn in a tax list, to disclose on oath the total amount of his taxable property. The court held that such a forced disclosure would violate the privilege against self-incrimination. But most of the prosecutions resulted in less sensational decisions, few were carried to the Court of Appeals, and most were settled before a fine was imposed.[9]

Naturally the county courts had a more intimate relationship with their own county levy, the basic source of the funds of county government. The tax commissioners obtained from heads of families the names of all tithables, a category which encompassed all males and female slaves sixteen years of age and older except those expressly exempted by the county courts "by reason of age, infirmity, or other charitable reasons." The commissioners turned the lists over to the sheriff, who was normally collector of the county levy. During a certain month, usually October or November, although for a time during May, a majority of the county magistrates held the claims court to settle claims and to set the county levy.[10]

In the form of a poll tax, the county levy was the same for everyone, old and young, rich and poor. Detractors crit-

[8] Fayette County Court Order Book, 1833–1836, p. 124 (U.K. microfilm, reel M366:5).

[9] Ibid., 1836–1840, pp. 281–83 (U.K. microfilm, reel M366:5); *Johnson* v. *Commonwealth*, 7 Dana 338 (1838).

[10] The basic statute concerning the county levy was enacted in 1797. *Acts, 1796–1797*, pp. 151–53.

icized it from time to time—most for its inherent unfairness
and some for its alleged unconstitutionality. The irascible
Humphrey Marshall questioned the validity of allowing
the county courts to levy a poll tax, arguing that the lower
house of the legislature possessed the exclusive right to
originate revenue bills and that it could not delegate this
authority. Although the Court of Appeals never heard this
question, it did rule some years after Marshall's accusation
that it was proper for the state to permit towns and cities to
tax and thereby seemingly scotched doubts about the validity of the county levy.[11]

Most critics dwelt on the unfairness of the tax. In his annual message to the legislature in 1827 Governor Joseph
Desha labelled it "wrong in principle and oppressive in
practice." He called it a "flagrant violation of principle" for
an undemocratic, "self-sustaining" body such as the county
court to "tax all, the rich and poor, precisely alike" and advocated the abolition of the tax and the substitution of an
ad valorem property assessment in its place. Supporters of
constitutional reform in the 1840s echoed the governor's
complaints, stressing particularly the argument against taxation without representation.[12]

In 1821 the legislature did limit the amount that the
county courts could levy as a poll tax to $1.50 per tithable,
but it never went so far as to abolish the tax as Desha recommended later. Again in January 1834 the General Assembly launched an inquiry into the feasibility of limiting
the poll tax to 50¢ per tithable and supplementing the loss
of revenue with an *ad valorem* tax on land and slaves; this
investigation was dropped less than one month later.[13]

[11] Humphrey Marshall, *History of Kentucky*, 2 vols., 2d ed. (Frankfort,
Ky., 1824), 2:218; *Talbot v. Dent*, 9 B. Monroe 526 (1849).

[12] *H.J., 1827–1828*, p. 20; *Convention*, 6 March 1847.

[13] *Acts, 1821*, chap. 342, sec. 2; *H.J., 1833–1834*, pp. 104–5, 249. In 1813 the
House narrowly defeated a proposal to repeal the poll tax. *H.J., 1812–1813*,
pp. 174–75.

Despite the existence of a maximum poll tax after 1821, the county courts raised substantial amounts of money from the levy. Indeed, George W. Kavanaugh, a delegate from Anderson County to the Constitutional Convention of 1849, estimated that the county courts collected "nearly as much money from the people as the legislature itself." Nor did the limitation on the amount of the tax prevent the courts from successfully petitioning the legislature for permission to exceed the maximum for special projects. These legislative authorizations varied in form: some simply increased the regular levy beyond the maximum amount, while others provided for an additional levy, usually of a certain amount, although sometimes open-ended. Occasionally the legislature expanded the levy, as for example in 1811 when it permitted the Fayette County Court to impose a two-dollar tax on all dogs "above two, kept or permitted to be kept upon any farm or plantation." During the height of turnpike construction certain county courts were authorized to supplement their regular levy by assessing an *ad valorem* tax on real property.[14]

One of the chronic problems of county taxation was the inability of some county courts to marshal a majority of their members to hold courts of claims and to assess the annual levy. The state statute books are filled with special acts authorizing county courts to levy delinquently or ratifying delinquent levies. The legislature from time to time investigated this shortcoming and in 1816 passed a law authorizing county courts to fine those magistrates who, without cause, failed to attend the court of claims.[15] Yet the numbers of county courts petitioning for extension of the time for levying or for ratification of late levies did not abate. In one instance the inability of a county court to summon a majority of its members caused acute embarrass-

14 *Proceedings*, p. 710; *Acts, 1810–1811*, chap. 278.
15 *Acts, 1815–1816*, chap. 385.

ment. In 1814 the Ohio County Court determined to lay the levy despite the fact that only half its members were present. An aggrieved taxpayer subsequently challenged the right of the sheriff to collect the tax and won a favorable decision in the circuit court; the county court was forced to assemble again and lay a new levy.[16] Yet in another case the high tribunal refused to invalidate a levy by the Owsley County Court simply because the levy exceeded the known claims against the county; this decision upheld an earlier ruling that the courts had wide discretion in levying and appropriating funds.[17]

Indeed some thought the courts had too much discretion in appropriation. A critic writing to the Frankfort *Kentucky Yeoman* in 1845 lamented the secrecy which surrounded the financial operations of the county courts and proposed that they open their books to the public or print their records in local newspapers. The present system, he argued, produced not a few incidents of fraud. Later a certain "W. P. D." endorsed these accusations, alleging that the justices of the Jessamine County Court had illegally appropriated funds from the county treasury to purchase law books for themselves after the legislature failed to pass a statute providing state money for the volumes. At the Constitutional Convention of 1849 George W. Kavanaugh noted that the county levy had not attracted "as much of the attention of the people as it should have," and John D. Taylor, delegate from Mason County, thanked God the levy could not "go beyond $1.50" per tithable.[18]

Most of the monies appropriated by the county courts were directed to four areas: roads and bridges, public build-

16 *Gilbert* v. *Huston,* Littell's Selected Cases 223 (1816).
17 *McGuire* v. *Justices of Owsley County,* 7 B. Monroe 340 (1847).
18 Frankfort *Kentucky Yeoman,* 11 December 1845 (hereafter cited as *Yeoman*); *Convention,* 27 March 1847; *Proceedings,* pp. 701, 710.

ings, the poor, and special salaries and fees. An examination of select budgets of five counties over the fifty-nine-year period of the old county court system reveals that these areas invariably consumed from approximately two-thirds to all of the annual county budgets.[19] Roads and bridges probably accounted for the greatest single expense, especially when investment in turnpike companies is added to the routine amounts delegated to upkeep of local roads. Until the great era of turnpike building commencing after the War of 1812, the courts were the principal agencies of road building and repair; thereafter the counties shared these responsibilities with semiprivate companies especially chartered to carve out macadamized roads.

The authority of the county courts to build and maintain roads derived from a system adopted by Virginians from English practice and codified by the Kentucky legislature in the form of the Public Road Law of 1797. The philosophy of road planning on the county level was individual initiative; that of road construction, alteration, and repair was self-help. In all phases the courts mediated rather than planned. The Public Road Law provided that the initiative for the proposal of local roads should come from the residents of the county rather than from the courts themselves. The statute specified that "when any person or persons" desired to have a road opened or altered to make more convenient "travelling to their county court house, or to any public ware-house, landing, ferry, mill, lead or iron-works, or the seat of government," they should apply to the county court, which would, in turn, appoint three or more fit persons to "view the ground along which such road is proposed to be conducted." They reported to the court

19 The county budgets examined and the years of the budgets were: Fayette, 1801, 1806, 1811, 1816, 1821, 1838; Bourbon, 1801, 1811, 1821, 1834, 1835; Christian, 1819, 1830, 1840; Estill, 1820, 1835, 1846; and Woodford, 1829, 1834, 1844. See the county court order books for these years.

which, if it decided the proposed road would be "convenient," summoned all "proprietors and tenants of the land" through which the proposed road would run to show cause why it should not be opened. The court then heard the complaints of the interested parties and issued a ruling on whether or not the road would be opened. Landowners opposing the road could demand that the court issue a writ of *ad quod damnum*, which initiated a common law procedure whereby a jury of twelve determined anew if the proposed road should be opened and, if so, what damages, if any, would be inflicted upon the complainant's property. If the jury determined that the proposed road was needed or if no one opposed the application and the county court found that a road was needed, the magistrates ordered the road built. If landowners affected by the approved road still felt aggrieved, they could appeal the county court's ruling to the Court of Appeals, which was empowered to try the case anew on both the facts and the law.[20]

Although it was apparently only infrequently exercised, the right of appeal was not an ineffective one. The Court of Appeals ruled in *Fletcher's Heirs* v. *Fugate* that an order of the Nicholas County Court establishing a road should be reversed since there had been no demonstration that public convenience would be served thereby. Furthermore, the court also determined that a county court could never withhold a writ of *ad quod damnum* from a person over whose land a proposed road was to run and that an order altering a road was reversible if all interested parties were not summoned. Yet it limited somewhat the right of judicial review by holding in *Taylor* v. *Brown* that a person challenging the

[20] The basic road law was passed in 1797. *Acts, 1796–1797*, pp. 157–62. In 1830 the legislature transferred the appellate jurisdiction under the road law from the Court of Appeals to the circuit courts, although the decision of the latter could, in most cases, be appealed to the former. *Acts, 1829–1830*, chap. 355.

establishment of a road must have a "direct" interest in the controversy.[21]

The method of building, altering, and maintaining local roads was also derived from English and Virginian custom. Each county court divided its county into precincts and over each appointed a "surveyor" or "overseer" whose duty it was to "superintend the road in his precinct." The number of surveyors varied from county to county and usually increased as the county court system matured. For example, in 1840 there were sixty-seven surveyors for Boone County, eighty-six for Washington, eighty-one for Garrard, and forty-five for Caldwell. The court "allotted hands" from each precinct to each surveyor. The supply of labor was ample since most males, black or white, sixteen years of age or older, were bound to work the roads without pay for as many days as necessary. Persons owning two or more slaves and heads of families with two or more male tithables were exempted on the assumption that the slaves or tithables would work the roads. Exemptions were also granted to persons fifty years or older or infirm and persons who provided a substitute not living in the precinct. Whenever a road was in need of repair, the surveyor and his hands were bound to repair it. Whenever a new road was to be built or an established one altered, the county court appointed a new surveyor and allotted him hands to do the work.[22]

The spirit of self-help manifested itself in other ways. Each laborer had to furnish his own tools. The surveyors, who were bound to keep the roads thirty feet wide, in good repair, and properly marked, were empowered to impound timber, earth, and stone from adjacent landowners and to impress carriages, draft horses or oxen, and drivers when

---

21 3 J. J. Marshall 631 (1830); *Peck* v. *Whitney*, 6 B. Monroe 117 (1845); *Walker* v. *Corn*, 3 A. K. Marshall 167 (1820); *Taylor* v. *Brown*, 3 Bibb 78 (1813).

22 *Acts, 1796–1797*, secs. 3–6, pp. 158–60.

needed. Two housekeepers valued the impounded mate-
rials and the court reimbursed the owner out of the county
levy.[23]

Not surprisingly, the county road system, especially the
element of forced free labor, was extremely controversial.
Critics cited numerous shortcomings and grievances. In his
annual message to the General Assembly in December 1810,
Governor Charles Scott accused the county courts of establishing too many roads and then neglecting them. The reason for this, he argued, was a division of authority. While
the county courts were authorized to establish roads and
appoint surveyors, the circuit courts retained complete authority to punish surveyors who failed to maintain the
roads. Others echoed and added to Scott's complaints. "A
Citizen of Fayette" in 1817 described the road system as
feudalistic, complained about being forced to work along-
side slaves, and implied that compulsory labor was unconstitutional. He contended that the roads in Fayette County
were impassable for six months of every year and advocated
a complete reform of the system to relieve the county courts
of the responsibility of establishing and maintaining roads
since they had "too much" to do anyway. The editor of the
Lexington *Kentucky Reporter*, writing in December 1829,
complained of "the wretched condition of our roads
throughout the winter and spring seasons of the year" despite the "large amount in both money and labor" which
was annually expended upon them. He accused the system
of discriminating against nonslaveholders and those living
near well-traveled roads, who were often required to spend
as many as forty days a year working for the precinct
surveyor.[24]

23 Ibid., secs. 4, 6.
24 *H.J., 1810–1811*, pp. 11–12; Lexington *Kentucky Gazette*, 13 December
1817 (hereafter cited as *Gazette*); Lexington *Kentucky Reporter*, 9 December
1829 (hereafter cited as *Reporter*).

These rumblings of discontent were eventually translated into efforts to reform. In 1830 the legislature enacted both a general law applicable to thirty counties and a specific law pertaining to Fayette County. The former statute was optional, granting to each county court the right to accept or reject it. If adopted, it provided for the annual election of three road commissioners who would form a corporate body which would supplant the county court as the chief instrument of road establishment and maintenance. The commissioners would be paid from $30 to $100 per year depending on the size of the county. Their salaries, plus funds for equipment and material, would be taken from an *ad valorem* tax on real property. Each white male adult over the age of sixteen would be liable to an annual poll tax not in excess of $1 which had to be paid in labor at a rate of 50¢ per day. Thus the system as reformed eliminated the impressment of supplies and material and curtailed sharply the period of forced labor.[25]

Obviously a compromise between those who desired to retain the old system and those who favored more basic reform, the general road law failed to alter profoundly and comprehensively the manner of establishing and maintaining roads because only a handful of county courts elected to adopt its provisions. Two counties, Bath and Woodford, adopted the law but soon after petitioned the legislature to revoke the new system and revive the old. Greenup County adopted the system, had the legislature revoke it in 1838, and then revived it again in 1845. Bracken, Mason, and Campbell were the only counties to adhere to the commissioner plan throughout the remaining twenty-one years of the old county court system.[26]

It was appropriate that the senator from Fayette County,

25 *Acts, 1829–1830*, chap. 332.

26 *Acts, 1830–1831*, chap. 393; *Acts, 1831–1832*, chap. 605; *Acts, 1837–1838*, chap. 638; *Acts, 1844–1845*, chap. 55.

Robert Wickliffe, Sr., successfully sponsored an act especially for his county since for years his constituents had been particularly agitated about the state of their roads. The Fayette statute was not optional; it was to go into effect as soon as the eligible voters elected three road commissioners at the annual election in August. The commissioners would form a corporate body, the Board of Public Works, to establish and maintain the county roads. They would serve for one-year terms and be paid $100 annually. An *ad valorem* tax on real property and a poll tax of 50¢ on all tithables would finance the expenses of the Board. Although taxpayers could work off their tax if they chose, the Fayette plan envisioned the hiring of most of the road labor. The only role reserved for the county court was the filling of vacancies should two or more of the commissioners resign from the Board.[27]

Senator Wickliffe wrote enthusiastically of the new system's virtues soon after its passage in a letter "to the freemen of the county." He submitted that the savings which would accrue from the elimination of forced labor and the impressment of material would more than offset the added tax burden. He also predicted that all the roads of the county would be macadamized, thereby stimulating the economy. Thus he respectfully solicited the support of his "countrymen" and reaffirmed his own, even though the new law would substantially increase his taxes.[28]

Wickliffe's entreaties were in vain, for although the Fayette citizenry harbored grievances against the old road system, it was soon apparent that they were unwilling to pay for a new one. The August elections, which attracted over 1,200 voters to the polls, produced only a handful of ballots for road commissioner. Wickliffe, upset and surprised by

27 *Acts, 1829–1830*, chap. 272.
28 *Reporter*, 17 February 1830.

the widespread opposition from a county which formerly had clearly voiced its dissatisfaction with the old road system, called for a meeting of his constituents for further "instructions."[29]

He must have gained new hope from that meeting, which was attended by the county's leading citizens—including Henry Clay, who normally remained aloof from county affairs—and which resulted in a statement of approbation for the new system. Some modifications to the plan were suggested, but they were slight: *per diem* rather than *per annum* pay for the commissioners and a temporary suspension of the operation of the law. Strangely enough, these proposed modifications were ignored, and when the legislature finally changed the law in January 1833 it simply raised the salaries of the road commissioners from $100 to $150 annually and directed that the law, which had yet to go into effect, be further suspended until August 1834.[30]

Meanwhile resistance to the new law accelerated, although isolated voices of support were heard. "Diogenes" wrote to the *Kentucky Reporter* in March 1832 that the roads in the county continued to be in poor condition and thus seriously disrupted the economy of the area. He depicted the old road system as "Gothic," accused the precinct surveyors of being too powerful, and lamented the delay in implementing the new law. Diogenes was a voice crying in the wilderness, for the elections of August 1834 again produced but a handful of votes for road commissioners. Soon afterward the justices of the county court in effect nullified the new road law by declaring that in their opinion the legislature had no constitutional authority to tamper with the road laws and that the court would "continue to exercise jurisdiction over the public highways of [the] county"

29 Ibid., 11 August, 8 September 1830.
30 Ibid., 13 October 1830; *Acts, 1832–1833*, chap. 181.

until the new law was declared valid by the "Highest Judicial Tribunall of the State." [31]

In September the three men who had received the highest number of votes for the office of road commissioner came into county court and refused to act in their new capacities, touching off a debate among the members of the tribunal and interested spectators on the validity of the new road law. Wickliffe led the fight for the law but obviously made little impression on the court, which voted unanimously to continue running the roads and did not suggest submitting the issue to a higher judicial body. The General Assembly, faced with a direct challenge to its authority by both the citizens and the court of Fayette County, capitulated at its next session and in short order approved a bill abolishing the new road system, which had never been implemented, and reviving the old. Thus ended the abortive effort to reform the road laws of one of the state's most prosperous and influential counties.[32]

The roads of Kentucky were not established exclusively by means of private initiative and application to the county courts. The General Assembly, in an early example of governmental planning, was also instrumental in authorizing road construction. Yet while the legislature sometimes approved proposed roads and occasionally funded parts of them, it normally relied upon the county courts to build and maintain them.

Normally state-authorized roads were intercounty, sometimes extending to the boundaries of the Commonwealth as part of an interstate route. The legislature usually appointed commissioners to view an authorized road and then delegated to the county courts the responsibility for fund-

[31] *Reporter*, 7 March 1832; Fayette County Court Order Book, 1833–1836, pp. 130–31 (U.K. microfilm, reel M366:5).

[32] Fayette County Court Order Book, 1833–1836, pp. 134–35, 141 (U.K. microfilm, reel M366:5); *Gazette*, 13 September 1834.

ing, building, and maintaining it. There were many variations in this pattern. Sometimes the General Assembly appointed county surveyors as commissioners to view a proposed route for a road; at other times it delegated to the county courts the responsibility of appointing these commissioners. In some plans the commissioners were to report to the legislature and in others to the county courts. Some statutes provided that the legislature should determine the expediency of implementing the commissioners' recommendations; others delegated this authority to the county courts; and still others made no provision, implying that the commissioners themselves should determine the expediency of building a road or that it had already been determined by the legislators. Normally once a route had been viewed, the county court was authorized to build the road, although occasionally state-appointed commissioners were assigned this task.[33]

Almost always the legislature provided that the county courts were to rely on the existing system of forced free labor or employ workers. Usually when the legislature specified that the work force was to be paid, it gave the courts the responsibility of funding the cost either out of the county levy or by means of private subscription, although on rare occasions the state paid for all or part of the construction. Even more rarely did the state assume the responsibility of maintaining roads; usually when it did, turnpikes were established and funds for maintenance were derived from tolls. Occasionally the legislature allotted funds to repair a county road, usually by means of land grants, and delegated complete authority over the project to commissioners. This usually occurred when the road ran through an economically distressed area.[34]

[33] See, for example, *Acts, 1830–1831*, chap. 464; *Acts, 1828–1829*, chap. 99, sec. 2; chap. 130, sec. 4; *Acts, 1826–1827*, chap. 77, sec. 3.

[34] See, for example, *Acts, 1821*, chap. 330.

The power of the county courts in road building receded after 1815 when state-chartered corporations began planning and constructing turnpikes. Normally the county courts had little, if anything, to do with the administration of turnpike companies, which were usually financed by both public and private funds and operated by private businessmen or local boards of internal improvements. Occasionally legislatively drawn company charters empowered certain county courts to condemn land for companies or to appoint and remove commissioners to sell stock subscriptions.[35] Even rarer was a provision such as the one in an act incorporating the Fayette and Madison Turnpike Company, which authorized the Fayette County Court to inspect the company's construction within the county.[36] Normally judicial supervision of private turnpike companies came from individual county magistrates or the circuit courts.

In the case of state roads converted into turnpikes by the legislature the role of county courts was more pronounced. For example, when the General Assembly made the Sandy Road a toll road in 1831, it authorized the relevant county courts to appoint and remove commissioners to manage and repair the turnpike in conjunction with the tribunals. The relationship of the county courts to the Wilderness Road, running from the Cumberland Gap to central Kentucky, evidences both the greater extent of participation of the tribunals in state-controlled turnpikes and the pragmatic, though often inconsistent, nature of state road policy. By virtue of a statute passed in 1805, the courts of those counties through which the road ran were given practically full control, including the duty to repair the road and the rights to appoint supervisory commissioners and to audit the accounts of the gatekeepers. In 1808 the legislature eliminated

---

35 *Acts, 1810–1811*, chap. 247; *Acts, 1834–1835*, chap. 865, sec. 3.
36 *Acts, 1817–1818*, chap. 284, sec. 13.

these powers and transferred the authority of the county courts to a board of directors to be appointed by the governor. In 1825 the legislature once again vested full power in the county courts to supervise and repair the turnpike, while three years later it transferred this authority to a superintendent to be appointed by the governor. In 1836 the legislature allowed certain county courts the privilege of appointing gatekeepers but revoked this authority two years later, giving it to state-appointed commissioners. Finally, in 1844 the General Assembly restored full power over the road to the county courts. It is apparent that throughout its dealings with the Wilderness Road the principal concern of the legislature was the effectiveness of management and maintenance rather than ideology or constitutional principles.[37]

Road surveyors and their allotted hands were bound to build and repair bridges and causeways, but it appears that most of them were unable to do so and that county courts contracted for much of this type of construction and maintenance.[38] Most frequently courts would appoint a special commissioner to "let and superintend" the building or repair of a bridge and would appropriate a specific sum of money to him for that purpose.[39] During the era of turnpike building some county courts contracted with turnpike companies or boards of internal improvements for the construction of bridges.[40]

37 *Acts, 1830–1831*, chap. 500; Littell, *Statute Law*, 3:282–87, 510–12; *Acts, 1824–1825*, chap. 190; *Acts, 1827–1828*, chap. 161; *Acts, 1835–1836*, chap. 294; *Acts, 1837–1838*, chap. 664; *Acts, 1843–1844*, chap. 328.

38 *Acts, 1796–1797*, sec. 7, p. 160.

39 In 1824 the Fayette County Court allocated $116 to a special commissioner to "let and supervise the rebuilding of the bridge across South Elkhorn." Fayette County Court Order Book, 1824–1827, p. 46 (U.K. microfilm, reel M366:3).

40 In 1836 the Scott County Court contracted with the Scott County Board of Internal Improvements to build a bridge over the North Elkhorn River;

Although following the War of 1812 the county courts relinquished to turnpike companies much of their domination over highway construction and had very little to do with the management of these enterprises, the local tribunals did contribute somewhat to their success. Not infrequently county courts purchased stock from newly formed companies; thus, while the courts seldom possessed powers of judicial or governmental control over the new agents of internal improvement, they maintained some leverage as investors.

The General Assembly often expressly encouraged county courts to invest in turnpike companies. It did this by incorporating local boards of internal improvements which were empowered to build turnpikes and authorizing the courts of those counties through which the roads would run to purchase stock in the corporations. It usually allowed the county courts to finance their stock purchases with an *ad valorem* tax on real property if the voters approved such a levy by petition. Some courts did not receive petitions and perhaps because of this chose not to purchase stock. Others purchased stock without receiving petitions, financing the investment either from the county levy or by assessing and collecting an *ad valorem* tax. Only a few levied an *ad valorem* tax and purchased stock after being duly petitioned.

The legislature did not always authorize county courts to purchase stock. This did not deter certain courts from investing, although there was some question about their constitutional right to do so. Some courts debated long and hard before deciding to purchase stock in turnpike companies and their decisions to do so sometimes generated considerable opposition. The Fayette County Court debated for over a year and frequently voted to postpone final

---

Scott County Court Order Book, 1831–1839, pp. 213, 382 (U.K. microfilm, reel M278:1842–43).

consideration of the question before deciding in February 1831 to subscribe to $15,000 worth of stock in the famous Maysville and Lexington Turnpike Company.[41]

The justices of Fayette were equally undecided over an effort between 1834 and 1836 by some of their members and other citizens of the county to have the court subscribe to substantial amounts of stock in five different turnpike companies. The justices may have been hesitant to pledge more of the county's funds to internal improvements since the Maysville Road had as yet failed to declare a dividend. In 1834 at the July and August courts the Fayette magistrates defeated by one vote motions to appropriate money to buy the turnpike stocks. Finally in June 1836 the justices agreed, with only one member dissenting, to purchase $15,500 worth of stock. While one local Whig newspaper, the Lexington *Intelligencer*, praised the court for its actions, William Boon, the senior magistrate of the court, who had cast the only negative vote, delivered a stinging criticism of the venture in the pages of the Democratic paper, the Lexington *Kentucky Gazette*. Boon decried the action of his fellow justices, arguing that it had been taken without once consulting the voters of the county and was based upon a usurpation of the Constitution. He contended that such activity on the part of the court violated the separation of powers clause and the legislature's exclusive right of taxation. Furthermore, he submitted, the expenditures illegally plunged the county into debt at a time when economy was needed. Boon's attack apparently created some uncertainty in the minds of his fellow justices, for they petitioned the legislature early at its next session to validate by statute

41 *Reporter*, 16 February 1831; Fayette County Court Order Book, 1827–1830, p. 304 (U.K. microfilm, reel M366:4). The courts of Nicholas and Bourbon counties also purchased stock in this venture but exhibited none of the indecision which clouded the Fayette deliberations. *H.J., 1832–1833*, pp. 52–53.

their decision to invest. The legislature complied in short order.[42]

Turnpike companies were not the only agencies of internal improvement aided by county courts. As railroads began to be proposed and built in Kentucky, county courts soon began purchasing stock in companies promoting this new form of transportation. Although many courts participated in railroading ventures without undue controversy or reverses, some encountered intense opposition and ultimate losses. The Fayette County Court's relationship with the abortive Louisville, Cincinnati and Charleston Railroad during the years 1836 to 1840 illustrates some of the dangers of government assistance to private enterprise in this period.

Backers of the Louisville, Cincinnati and Charleston Railroad predicted that the construction of their line, which would connect the Ohio Valley with the Carolina coast, would produce new markets and wealth for both Kentucky and the South. Business and political leaders of Lexington, anxious to revitalize the city's economic position, which had been declining since the advent of the steamboat, eagerly championed the railroad and urged the governments of the city and county to purchase a sizeable amount of the company's stock on the condition that the line would terminate in Kentucky at the capital of the bluegrass region rather than at Louisville. As inducement the Fayette representatives to the General Assembly secured an amendment to the company's charter providing that Lexington would be the railroad's Kentucky terminus.[43] Furthermore, the directors of the railroad had promised that

---

[42] Fayette County Court Order Book, 1833–1836, pp. 113, 122; Fayette County Court Order Book, 1836–1840, p. 28 (U.K. microfilm, reel M366:5); Lexington *Intelligencer*, 14 June 1836 (hereafter cited as *Intelligencer*); *Gazette*, 25 July 1836; *Acts, 1836–1837*, chap. 7.

[43] *Acts, 1836–1837*, chap. 387, sec. 2.

construction would begin at Lexington. Swayed by these diligent promotions, the Fayette County Court voted in December 1836 to subscribe to $100,000 worth of railroad stock on condition of legislative approval and authorization to impose an *ad valorem* tax on real property, which was forthcoming in January.[44]

The enormity of the stock subscription, the fact that the venture was highly speculative and undersubscribed, the failure of either the court or the legislature to require an endorsement from the voters, and the unprecedented inauguration of a county tax on real property perhaps made it inevitable that the court's action would arouse fierce opposition within the county.[45] By late March 1837 the *Kentucky Gazette,* edited by Daniel Bradford, a county magistrate who had eagerly supported the court's promise to purchase the stock, could report that "much discontent [was] being manifested from different parts of Fayette, on account of the subscriptions by the county court, for stock in the rail road."[46] Bradford speculated that the court would soon order a special election to ascertain the will of the people on the issue.

Within three weeks organized opposition to the stock subscription had manifested itself at a meeting in Chilesburgh, headquarters of one of the county's four election precincts. Participants in the meeting resolved that the stock subscription was "an outrage and usurpation of power, unauthorized by the Constitution." They called upon two prominent citizens of the area, one of whom was Jacob Hughes, a large landholder, to become candidates for the legislature, an action which suggests that they wanted the two men to seek the repeal of the statute validating the court's subscription. They also urged citizens of the Athens

44 Ibid., chap. 121.
45 *Gazette,* 15 December 1836; *Intelligencer,* 8 August 1837.
46 *Gazette,* 30 March 1837.

and Elkhorn precincts to meet and make known their views on the court's "unconstitutional appropriation."[47]

Meanwhile supporters of subscription rallied to the cause of the county court. In a letter to the *Gazette* "a Subscriber" accused certain "politicians" from the Chilesburgh precinct of attempting "to thwart the measure and to disgrace their county court" and argued that even if the subscription had been entered into illegally, it should be upheld because of the honor of the county and the reliance "interested parties" placed upon it. Nine days after the Chilesburgh meeting the citizens of the Athens precinct met and issued a series of resolutions endorsing the actions of the county magistrates. The meeting "deemed it of vital importance to the prosperity of this State, that the great work, which is designed to connect the valley of the west with the Atlantic Ocean, . . . should be immediately commenced" and should receive not only the financial support of Fayette County but also of all counties through which the proposed railroad was to run as well as the state itself.[48]

Buoyed by these demonstrations of support, the county court justices at first rejected a proposed public vote on the issue. Nonetheless they were sufficiently uncertain about the soundness of their proposed investment to order a delay in levying the newly authorized tax on real property until it was determined that the railroad company had accepted the amendments to its charter passed by the recent legislature and that all monies appropriated by the court would be expended within the county. At its June term the court, without apparent knowledge of the company's response to its inquiries, reversed itself and authorized both the collection of the tax to make the first payment on the subscription and a public referendum in August "to take the sense of the people of the county, whether they are for or against forfeit-

47 Ibid., 27 April 1837.
48 Ibid., 4 May 1837.

ing the stock, after making the first payment." This was a shrewd political maneuver, for obviously the justices were attempting to force even the most frugal citizen to vote for the subscription by converting the question from one of honoring a contract to one of forfeiture of funds already expended. Not only the "honor" of the county was at stake, but also $5,000.[49]

Between June and the August election these questions were hotly debated by the people of Fayette County. In an eloquent letter to the *Gazette* a farmer from Chilesburgh, signing himself "a Friend to the Constitution," defended his precinct's remonstrance, arguing that he and his neighbors were simply trying to stem the excesses of local government. "Lycurgus" replied that the economic welfare of the county was indeed at stake and called for the voters not only to endorse the subscription but also to reject Jacob Hughes, the legislative candidate of the opposition. Hughes, the only candidate who was identified with the antisubscription forces, equivocated when called upon to commit himself by replying that while he generally favored the concept of the Charleston Railroad, he likewise warmly endorsed the right of the people to instruct their county court on such matters.[50]

Shortly before the elections proponents of the railroad held a series of meetings throughout the county in an effort to rally their supporters. Their endeavors were not in vain, for the voters endorsed the subscription by a margin of more than two to one. Oddly enough, the Athens precinct voted nearly two to one against the county court, while Chilesburgh not surprisingly opposed the measure 87 votes to 61. The Lexington city precinct ultimately carried the question, voting 1,095 to 435 in favor of subscription. The

---

[49] Fayette County Court Order Book, 1836–1840, pp. 92, 161 (U.K. microfilm, reel M366:5).

[50] *Gazette*, 22 June, 27 July 1837; *Intelligencer*, 25 July, 1 August 1837.

voters also elected the four prosubscription candidates to the legislature and rejected Jacob Hughes, the noncommital standard bearer of the opposition.[51]

This victory at the polls, however, did not make the Fayette County Court's investment any more secure. Robert Wickliffe, Sr., representing the court at the railroad's executive meeting in November at Charleston, sounded a warning when he wrote that federal support of the venture would not be forthcoming. In May 1838 the situation appeared so bleak that some advocated forfeiture. The court voted to postpone the next levy until the railroad again produced satisfactory evidence that it intended to spend all Fayette funds within the county. In August representatives from the railroad came before the court and made the requisite pledge. The following month, apparently satisfied that the railroad was still viable, the justices voted to impose the tax and pay the second installment. Shortly thereafter Daniel Bradford exuded confidence in the project and called for the opposition to cease their bickering and "submit like republicans to the wish of the county."[52]

Unfortunately Bradford's optimism proved ill-founded. In November 1838 the leaders of the city and county called a public meeting on the subject of the railroad. Although the proceedings were never publicized, it is apparent that a crisis was at hand. At the May term of 1839 the assembled magistrates once again heard a report by representatives of the railroad, but this time they rejected the company's pledge of good faith. The court informed the railroad that it would meet the next installment only when it was demonstrated conclusively that construction would soon commence within the county. There is no evidence that the

51 *Intelligencer*, 28 July, 11 August 1837.
52 *Gazette*, 23 November 1837, 10 May, 13 September 1838; Fayette County Court Order Book, 1836–1840, pp. 268–69, 311–12 (U.K. microfilm, reel M366:5).

railroad ever reported to the court again. By September the situation was so hopeless that the court ordered over $1,000 in a "surplus railroad fund" to be transferred to a fund for a new clerk's office. During the next three years the Fayette court made repeated but unavailing attempts to regain all or part of the $10,000 it had invested in the railroad. Poor planning, formidable geographical obstacles, and lack of governmental and private financial support had rendered the Louisville, Cincinnati and Charleston Railroad insolvent and forever lifeless.[53]

The county courts performed vital functions for the Commonwealth in the levying and collection of taxes and the building and maintenance of roads. They also made a substantial financial contribution to the state's program of internal improvements. Yet their operation in these sensitive economic areas aroused considerable official and popular opposition, which contributed to the growing insecurity of the courts in the political system of the state. The response of their members to the state's first two-party system was to have the same effect.

[53] *Gazette,* 22 November 1838; Fayette County Court Order Book, 1836–1840, pp. 389, 415; Fayette County Court Order Book, 1840–1846, pp. 20, 108–9, 189 (U.K. microfilm, reels M366:5–6).

Chapter 4

THE POLITICS
OF THE COUNTY COURTS

I T IS NOT SURPRISING that spirited battles were fought to secure control of the county courts, whose power resided not only in their combination of executive, judicial, and legislative functions but also in their ability to fill their own vacancies and in their domination of almost all local patronage. Indeed a major part of county political warfare was waged to secure appointments to the courts. It will be recalled that whenever a vacancy occurred on a county court, the Constitution of 1799 provided that a majority of the justices of the peace should recommend two persons to the governor and that he should select one of them as the replacement. Many appointments under this system were strictly routine matters taking place without controversy: normally governors selected the person recommended first since he was usually the first choice of the tribunal. However, the governor was not constitutionally bound to commission the court's first choice, and this discretionary factor gave dissident groups opportunities to challenge the action of county courts by promoting the merits of second choices. Early in the history of the old county court system extraconstitutional devices began to influence appointments to the courts. Petitions and letters were the two most frequently used means to put pressure on both courts and governors. Petitions to the courts normally

urged the recommendation of specific persons to fill vacancies. Petitions and letters to the governor not infrequently
cited unusual circumstances which would allow the commissioning of the candidate recommended second.

The germination of Kentucky's first two-party system in
1827 increased the use of old methods and produced new
and more sophisticated ways to influence decisions affecting
the patronage of the county courts. Petitions and letters
continued to be utilized and grew in quantity and quality.
For example, one petition from Bracken County sent to
Governor John Breathitt in 1833 included the party affiliation of each of the signatories to establish its bipartisan
flavor.[1] Letters grew longer and more detailed, and in some
cases correspondents wrote more than once if the contest
was especially crucial or heated. Letter writers wrote not
only for themselves but also for relatives, friends, and in
many cases allegedly for the "most respected" citizens of
their communities. In some instances important men in
Frankfort were used as references. Public meetings and
party pollings were added to these traditional instruments
of political pressure. Where competition for office was especially keen, rival parties sometimes held meetings or elections or both to furnish evidence of support for their
respective candidates and then sent the results to both the
county courts and the governor. Each camp inevitably
branded as unrepresentative the other's meetings and pollings, yet these devices seem to have had some effect on the
outcome of the most bitter patronage fights. The courts
themselves, or rather factions of them, and certain governors also devised novel methods to meet the new realities
of two-party politics. Parties or factions occasionally used
rump sessions of courts to seize power; since governors were
generally unwilling to challenge apparently valid orders

[1] Petition to Governor John Breathitt (ca. 1833), Breathitt Papers (G.P.,
reel 37).

from county courts these tactics were often successful. Furthermore, courts and governors on occasion openly solicited public applications for court vacancies or expressions of public sentiment regarding persons recommended.

Before 1827 most politicians of Kentucky were Jeffersonians or Democratic-Republicans. In 1820 two loosely knit factions emerged around the relief issue, a "Relief" or "New Court" party and an "Anti-Relief" or "Old Court" party, but they were too unorganized to be regarded as political parties.[2] Most of the battles over patronage which occurred before a well-defined two-party system emerged were conducted on an ad hoc basis and were essentially personality contests. Candidates before the county courts and nominees of the courts were supported or opposed on the basis of their reputations, competence, or place of residence rather than their commitment to party or program. Yet there is some indication that in a few early instances factions or "party spirit" entered into patronage disputes in some counties. "Party prejudice" was so intense in Bracken County at the beginning of the nineteenth century that the two senior justices of the peace on the court refused to serve as sheriff, and a third person who had "not taken an active part in [the] county scuffle" was appointed. In 1815 opposition was unsuccessfully raised to the first choice of the Warren County Court for justice of the peace on the grounds that the candidate possessed "federal or Tory principles" and had threatened to move to Canada rather than fight in the War of 1812. A correspondent of Governor John Adair writing in May 1820 revealed that "great efforts [were] made by a factious party in Todd county" to place its candidate first in nomination for justice of the peace and that for several weeks before the court met there

---

[2] Richard P. McCormick, *The Second American Party System: Party Formation in the Jacksonian Era* (Chapel Hill, N.C., 1966), pp. 212–16.

was much "planning and plotting." This activity was in vain, however.[3]

The presidential campaign of 1828 saw the commencement of the first viable two-party system in the state. In late 1827 and early 1828 supporters of John Quincy Adams and Andrew Jackson each held county and state meetings designed to drum up support for their candidates. The pro-Adams group, which was also partial to Henry Clay, referred to itself by a number of names, including "the People's Ticket," and the Jacksonians likewise claimed various appellations, including "Republican." In 1834 the anti-Jacksonian party became known as the Whig Party, whereas the Jacksonians were most commonly referred to as Democrats.[4]

The introduction of well-organized political parties changed the nature of patronage struggles in the counties. The stakes of power began to increase; the problem of who would fill a vacancy on a county court came to be not only a matter of local personalities but also a question of which party would control the court. In many counties newly born political parties immediately seized control of county courts and assiduously maintained and solidified their domination. Which party controlled a county court was often fortuitous, and not infrequently that control did not correspond to the wishes of the body politic. Indeed the courts' power of self-perpetuation immunized them in many ways from democratic pressures. In some counties parties which seldom won at the polls were firmly entrenched in the county courts. Thus even though they could not elect rep-

[3] Petition to Governor James Garrard (ca. 1802), Garrard Papers, jacket 28 (G.P., reel 7); Obadiah Hendricks to Governor Isaac Shelby, 14 July 1815, Shelby Papers, jacket 128 (G.P., reel 16); (Unknown) to Governor John Adair, 11 May 1820, Adair Papers, jacket 216 (G.P., reel 24).

[4] Leonard P. Curry, "Election Year: Kentucky, 1828," *Register, Kentucky State Historical Society* 55 (July 1957): 196–212.

resentatives either to the state legislature or to Congress, they could control the local government and much of the local patronage.

Fayette was a county wherein a political party largely unsuccessful at the ballot box, the Jacksonian Democrats, dominated the county court. This control originated largely by chance. In 1827 the Jacksonians happened to have a narrow majority on the court. Not wishing to risk a shift in the balance of power, during the next two decades they generally proscribed members of the opposition party. By 1831 the Democrats had attained a solid majority and had caused a pro-Clay newspaper of the county, the *Kentucky Reporter,* to portray the county magistrates as an "irresponsible body of aristocrats," an epithet commonly thought to have been reserved only for anti-Jacksonians but in reality freely employed by members of both antebellum political parties. Although the *Reporter* threatened "a day of retribution" and predicted an outburst of "public indignation," the unperturbed Jacksonians continued to bolster their majority until by 1845 only three Whigs were on the Fayette court of twenty-two justices of the peace.[5]

The situation in Fayette County was hardly unusual. Of twenty sample courts, five were controlled by members of a party largely unsuccessful at the polls.[6] In one county, Harrison, the Whigs ruled the local tribunal, while Democrats normally won the elective offices. In four others, Fayette, Montgomery, Woodford, and Franklin, the Democrats dominated the county court while the Whigs customarily prevailed at the ballot box. The Franklin County Court was not only controlled by a Democratic party generally unsuccessful at the polls but also gave evidence of nepotism.

[5] *Reporter,* 27 July 1831.

[6] The twenty counties studied were Bourbon, Clark, Estill, Fayette, Franklin, Garrard, Grant, Harrison, Henry, Jefferson, Jessamine, Madison, Mason, Montgomery, Nicholas, Pendleton, Scott, Shelby, Wayne, and Woodford.

The McKee family and its in-laws at one time furnished
four of the county court's thirteen justices of the peace and
four of its nine constables, as well as the county surveyor.
This political inbreeding finally provoked a public outburst in 1843 in the form of petitions asserting that the
McKee family had such a "preponderating influence in the
county court that they nominate for magistrates and appoint as constables their own relatives wholly disregarding
the public interest or public wish." Nepotism was not an
isolated characteristic of Franklin County. In a single year
nine appointees to justice of the peace positions listed in
Governor Joseph Desha's journal bore the same last names
as their predecessors and James P. Hamilton, delegate from
Larue County, declared at the Constitutional Convention
of 1849 that "with very few exceptions, every magistrate had
a son or a son-in-law riding under him." [7]

Unrepresentative party domination and nepotism were
not the only cankers weakening the county court structure
in Kentucky. Party bossism was also widespread. In Brack-
en County, petitioners residing in the town of Augusta complained to the governor in the fall of 1833 that their preference for justice of the peace was ignored by the county
court because of the machinations of the county attorney,
whom they characterized as having "almost unlimited influence . . . with the majority of said Court." The petitioners went on to accuse the county attorney, the leader of the
county's Clay party, "of putting in what men he chooses"
and branded his choice for office as a man whose principles
smacked of "Federalism." Apparently these charges of "aristocratic influence" sat well with Governor John Breathitt,
a Jacksonian, for he commissioned the petitioners' first
choice and the court's second, one Samuel Keene, a fellow

---

7 *Commonwealth*, 8 August 1843; Petition to Governor Robert Letcher
(ca. February 1843), Letcher Papers, jacket 482 (G.P., reel 73); Journal of
Governor Joseph Desha, 1824–1828, pp. 295, 299–300, 303, 324, 339, 417, 450–
51 (G.P., reel 27); *Proceedings*, p. 705; *Convention*, 6 March 1847.

Jacksonian. In 1835 Whigs accused Worden Pope, leader of the Democratic party in Louisville, of dominating the Jefferson County Court, an allegation which was hotly denied by the Democrats.[8]

While partisan control in most counties, such as Fayette, Franklin, and Clay, accompanied the beginning of the two-party system, some courts did not evidence one-party domination until as late as the 1840s. In Campbell County, Democrats and Whigs on the court were evenly divided until November 1840. At that time the Democrats gained a majority by declaring a Whig seat vacant because of the prolonged absence of its occupant from the county and filling it with a fellow Jacksonian. Although prominent Whigs protested, the Democratic coup in Campbell County was sanctioned by the governor, who, despite his allegiance to the Whig cause, was reluctant to tamper with the official proceedings of the court.[9] Six years later Breathitt County Democrats made an even more spectacular seizure of power. At the outset of their maneuverings in July 1846 Democrats were a minority of six, Whigs held seven seats, and there were two vacancies. All six Democrats assembled, with only one Whig in attendance, and proceeded to fill the two vacancies with Jacksonians, notwithstanding the objections of the Whig. The recommendations were adhered to by the governor, although he himself was a Whig and despite the fact that the Constitution required a majority of the members of the court to agree to all recommendations. Again the reluctance of Kentucky's governors to countermand official-looking county court orders apparently explains the success of the Democratic rump sessions.[10]

8 Petitions and letters to Governor John Breathitt, Breathitt Papers (G.P., reel 37); Louisville *Public Advertiser*, 13 February 1835.

9 Benjamin D. Beale to Governor Robert Letcher, 10 November 1840, Letcher Papers, jacket 390 (G.P., reel 56).

10 For an account of the Democratic coup in Breathitt County see the petition of the seven Whig justices of the peace to Governor William Owsley

In light of the extent of one-party domination of county courts, it is not surprising that after 1827 most of the patronage battles of county government involved either entrenched parties seeking to preserve their positions of dominance or "out" parties seeking to gain control of the court. Of course many one-party courts obviated interparty patronage fights by taking care to recommend as their second choice for vacated magistracies candidates who were fully as acceptable as the first choice, but this was not always the case. Sometimes partisan tribunals recommended as second choices members of out parties, doubtless confident that their first choices would be commissioned. Such strategy could lead to interparty confrontation, especially when the court's first choice was vulnerable on ethical grounds. For example, not long after the Democrats seized control of the Campbell County Court by means of a rump session, a bitter dispute arose from their efforts to solidify their new control by filling a vacancy with a loyal party member. The controversy opened at the June 1847 term of the court when the Democratic majority recommended that Robert D. Hayman, a former justice of the peace and an acting trustee of the town of Newport, be appointed a magistrate with another Newportian, A. Boyd, the second choice. Hayman's recommendation elicited a powerful objection from three citizens of Newport who, in a letter to Governor William Owsley, accused Hayman of being insane. They urged the appointment of Boyd, ostensibly a Democrat, or a third candidate, a Whig named H. A. Mayo, who had previously been rejected by the court. Owsley was apparently impressed by this accusation and named Boyd to the court.

The Campbell court was not to be permanently overruled, however. In December 1847 the court again picked Hayman to fill a recent vacancy, and this time it prepared

(ca. July 1846) and a copy of the order of the county court in the Owsley Papers, jacket 620 (G.P., reel 89).

itself for the challenges which were sure to come. Partisans for Hayman held meetings and elections, circulated petitions, and wrote letters upholding his sanity and denouncing his detractors. His enemies adopted similar tactics, holding their own rallies and polls and circulating contrary petitions. This time their letters to the governor accused Hayman not only of being insane but also of beating his wife and children, of being so dangerous and feared that defendants would default rather than appear before him in magistrate's court, and of being so partisan that no Whig could ever obtain a fair trial from him. Although his enemies sometimes pretended that their candidate for the vacancy and the court's second choice, one L. M. Eckert, was a Democrat, it was frankly admitted by some that he had turned Whig in recent years. It also became clear that Boyd was really a Whig. Thus strong overtones of partisan politics as well as personalities unquestionably influenced the struggle. This time Governor Owsley gave in to the Democrats and commissioned Hayman, the alleged "monomaniac." [11]

Usually governors would reject first choices for justice of the peace only on moral grounds or proof of incompetence. In 1841 the Whig voters of the Ghent region of Carroll County endeavored to secure the commissioning of their court's second choice, also a Whig, to fill a vacancy. The governor rejected this attempt and commissioned the tribunal's first choice, a Democrat, since the petitioners could offer no reason for overturning the court's preference other than partisan feelings.[12]

Often parties in control of county courts did not attempt to counteract public pressure on the governor to overturn partisan first choices for justice of the peace. They simply

[11] Ibid., jackets 651, 705.

[12] Notation by Governor Robert Letcher on petition from citizens of Carroll County, 2 March 1841, Letcher Papers, jacket 408 (G.P., reel 59).

relied on the authority of their orders and on precedent, a strategy which usually proved successful even under the most vigorous opposition. In 1846 the Democratic majority on the Green County Court ignored pleas of residents of the Brush Creek region to recommend a justice of the peace from their area, which had long been unrepresented. Instead the court successfully suggested the appointment of a fellow Democrat who, although he lived far from the Brush Creek area, had campaigned assiduously for the office. The decision of the Jacksonians was undoubtedly made easier by the fact that the Brush Creek residents supported a Whig for the office.[13]

On other occasions parties firmly in control of county courts unwittingly provoked patronage fights by adopting procedures normally utilized by out parties. In February 1843 the solidly Whig Mason County Court offered to allow a neighborhood in which a vacancy on the court had occurred to indicate its preference for a replacement by means of an election. The court was doubtless confident that the voters of the area, overwhelmingly Whig, would choose one of the party faithful, especially since two of the three candidates were Democrats. Much to the court's chagrin, one of the Democrats, David R. Bullock, received more votes than the other Democrat and the Whig together. At the April term the court indicated that it would ignore the results of the election, an action which prompted Bullock's followers to submit a petition of support allegedly signed by nearly every eligible voter, including all those not participating in the election. At its May term the court remained adamant and overwhelmingly endorsed the Whig candidate, "tittering in a jocular manner" that Bullock "was a good Democrat." Bullock himself then wrote to Governor Letcher denouncing the court's action and characterizing his Whig

13 Owsley Papers, jacket 566 (G.P., reel 84).

opponent as most unpopular because of "his profanity and gamblin habits." Despite these protestations, Letcher commissioned the court's first choice.[14]

Party infighting was so rampant in some counties that efforts were occasionally made to seek apolitical appointments to the court. In 1843 certain members of the Clay County Court, believing that the presence of excessive "party spirit" on the tribunal made it "impossible sometimes to do any business at all," convened secretly to nominate for vacancies "men who [were] both independant and independant in their manner of doing business." Despite objections from those undoubtedly infected with excessive "party spirit," Governor Letcher acquiesced in the court's purge.[15]

Some disputes over patronage on the county level did not involve partisan conflict. This was generally true of attempts by people living in unrepresented areas of counties to secure justices of the peace. The problem of geographical apportionment of magistrates was acute in many counties, and not a few so-called districts of counties claimed to be underrepresented or not represented at all.[16] It was generally believed that there was no constitutional obligation on the part of county courts to distribute magistrates in an equitable geographical fashion, and one governor vetoed a bill which would have compelled the Ohio County Court to name a justice of the peace from a certain district in the county.[17] Faced with this constitutional obstacle and with the necessity of settling the many petty legal disputes which

[14] David R. Bullock to Governor Robert Letcher, 5 May 1843, Letcher Papers, jacket 471 (G.P., reel 70).

[15] Samuel Ensworth to Governor Robert Letcher, 6 July 1843, and other relevant documents in the Letcher Papers, jacket 481 (G.P., reel 73).

[16] Regions of counties calling themselves "districts" were evidently referring to their constabulary districts, subdivisions of each county. Littell, *Statute Law*, 2:35.

[17] *H.J., 1844–1845*, pp. 146–47.

plague all civilized societies, and possessed of the desire for representation on the principal agency of county government, many regions were forced to beseech both court and governor to fill their needs for local magistrates.

Most of these requests for magistrates were void of references to party politics, confining themselves to the issue of representation. Typical is the response of a citizen living in the western end of Anderson County. In a letter to Governor Letcher written on March 15, 1842, John Wash complained that his region had never had a magistrate since the formation of the county in 1827. He recounted that after several petitions to the court had failed to gain relief, the inhabitants sought a law from the General Assembly creating two additional justices of the peace for the county. The legislature granted this request but of course could not specify the location of the new magistrates. Predictably, citizens of the town of Lawrenceburg, the population center and county seat, pressured the court into recommending men from their locale to fill the new offices. Residents of the western end protested to both the court and the governor, but to no avail.[18]

In Logan County the sins of the county court were even more serious. In 1845 when a vacancy occurred on the court after its senior magistrate, David T. Smith, was named sheriff, a region in the county petitioned for a justice of the peace, claiming none had resided there for many years. Instead of granting the petition, the court delayed filling the vacancy until two years later, when Smith's term as sheriff expired, and then in a rump session recommended that he be appointed a justice of the peace again. Irate residents of the unrepresented district threatened to support a constitutional modification of the entire county court system if redress were not forthcoming. On this occasion Governor

18 John Wash to Governor Robert Letcher, 15 March 1842, Letcher Papers, jacket 433 (G.P., reel 63).

Owsley refused to abide by the court's recommendation and ultimately commissioned the preference of the aggrieved neighborhood.[19]

Regional disgruntlement over lack of representation on a county court sometimes led to measures more extreme than simple petitions to the governor for reapportionment. Citizens of the southern part of Mercer County in and around Danville were so chagrined by the alleged discrimination of their county court that in 1834 they commenced petitioning the legislature to create a new county out of their region so that they might manage their own affairs. They accused the Mercer court of fostering taxation without representation, conducting fraudulent elections, and favoring in fiscal matters the county seat of Harrodsburg at the expense of Danville. Underlying the frustration of those in south Mercer was their overwhelming sympathy toward the anti-Jacksonian party, while their more numerous brethren in the north were equally partisan toward the Democrats. This "basic disagreement politically . . . on the leading topics of national policy" had produced "frequent and violent altercations" and a proscription of the south Mercerians from membership on the county court.[20] After eight years of petition and counterpetition, in which the dissidents advocated constitutional secession, the legislature finally authorized the divorce of the south from the north and the formation of Boyle County.[21]

Complementing the tendency of Kentucky's county courts to be dominated by a political party or faction was

[19] George J. Blakey to Governor William Owsley, 22 March 1847, and E. A. Hawkins to Owsley, 24 May 1847, Owsley Papers, jacket 650 (G.P., reel 94); see also *Convention*, 22 May 1847.

[20] *Intelligencer*, 23 September 1834, 23 January 1835.

[21] *Acts, 1841–1842*, chap. 189. The convoluted story of the origins of Boyle County may be traced in the *Commonwealth*, 18 February 1842; *H.J., 1834–1835*, pp. 63, 69, 144, 181, 201, 208, 301, 360; *S.J., 1835–1836*, p. 157; *H.J., 1837–1838*, pp. 66, 80, 103, 211, 231; *H.J., 1840–1841*, pp. 177, 390; *H.J., 1841–1842*, pp. 74, 135, 167, 171; *S.J., 1841–1842*, pp. 213, 233, 253, 260, 275, 283, 287.

the inclination of their members to serve actively in party politics during the formative years of the state's two-party system. Newspaper accounts of political meetings in twenty of the state's counties and newspaper lists of delegates to state political conventions from the same counties indicate that in sixteen of them, from one-half to all of the county court's members were active participants in one of the two major parties.[22] In half of the counties studied, from two-thirds to all of the members of the courts as of 1837 had taken part in one or more county political meetings and state political conventions. In six other counties from one-half to two-thirds of the members were similarly involved. In only four counties did fewer than half of the magistrates actively participate in party matters.

Not infrequently county magistrates were outright leaders of local party organizations. For example, a justice of the peace was either chairman or some other officer of all ten Democratic party meetings held in Fayette County from 1827 to 1848. Fifteen of twenty-five members of the county's Democratic vigilance committee in 1840 were either current or former members of the county court. In Woodford County acting or retired magistrates chaired five of six reported Democratic meetings and five of eight Whig meetings from 1827 to 1848. At a meeting in 1831 of the Jacksonian partisans of Montgomery County, twenty of fifty delegates were either retired, active, or future magistrates, and at the 1827 conclave of Jacksonians in Scott County

22 See note 6 for a list of the counties studied. These were the only counties in the state for which a sufficient number of party lists were available for both Jacksonians and anti-Jacksonians. Newspapers containing lists of participants at county political meetings and state conventions and accounts of other party events include: Frankfort *Argus of the Western World*, 1830–1831, 1835–1836; *Commonwealth*, 1834–1836, 1839, 1843, 1846–1848; *Gazette*, 1827–1828, 1834–1836, 1839–1840, 1842–1843; *Reporter*, 1827–1831; Lexington *Observer and Reporter*, 1834, 1836, 1839–1840, 1847–1848 (hereafter cited as *Observer and Reporter*); *Yeoman*, 1847–1848; and Louisville *Daily Journal*, 1842.

nine of the twenty-one delegates and members of the committee of correspondence were or soon would be justices of the peace.[23]

Those justices who were the most vigorous politicians tended to be members of a county court dominated by one of the two major parties. The courts of Bourbon, Fayette, Franklin, Garrard, Grant, Harrison, Jessamine, Montgomery, Scott, and Woodford counties were controlled by either Whig or Democratic majorities, all of whom were energetic members of their county and state party organizations. In contrast, members of bipartisan county courts tended to be politically inactive. The justices of the peace in Nicholas, Jefferson, and Madison counties were only moderately active, while those of Henry, Clark, Estill, and Wayne were relatively inactive—the only inactive counties among the twenty examined.[24] Finally, it should be noted that in four of the seven county courts with bipartisan membership, neither political party monopolized the elections, while in the thirteen counties in which courts were controlled by one party the elections were also clearly one-sided.

Not only were many of the justices of the county courts political leaders in their own right, but also they controlled much of the state's election machinery. Throughout the period of the old county court system, the local tribunals appointed a majority of the county's principal election offi-

[23] *Gazette*, 12 October, 23 November, 28 December 1827; 15 March, 12 April, 14 June, 22 November 1834; 17 October 1839; 12 March 1840; 15 October 1842; 18 November 1843. Frankfort *Argus of Western America*, 24 September 1828; 14, 21 December 1831; 10 February 1836. *Reporter*, 14 November 1827; 17 November 1830; 9 November 1831. *Commonwealth*, 15 June, 10 November 1847; 18 February 1848.

[24] An active court is defined as one in which from two-thirds to all of the members were publicly involved in the party system, a moderately active court as one in which from one-half to two-thirds of the membership were involved, and a relatively inactive court as one in which fewer than half of the members were involved.

cials, including two judges and a clerk. Partisan feelings doubtless influenced the execution of responsibilities by courts and judges alike since at least during the two-party period some counties regularly reported more votes than legal voters. In 1842 the legislature sought to remedy this practice by declaring that wherever possible county courts were to choose one judge from each party, yet complaints of undue partisanship persisted.[25]

Both antebellum political parties, the Jacksonian Democrats and the Whigs, defended and profited from the essentially oligarchical structure of county politics. Both sides had their share of "aristocrats," a term defined here in part as an epithet used by a member of one party coveting a county office held by a member of the other party. This tradition of bipartisan oligarchy seriously undercuts the notion of a spirit of democracy which supposedly prevailed during the age of Jackson and which was allegedly monopolized by members of his party.

County court politics provides colorful evidence of the ingenuity of politicians in the area of extraconstitutional creativity. The abundance of petitions, letters, public meetings, unofficial elections, and even rump sessions of court created a significant expansion of the formal appointive procedures established for county government. This same spirit, of course, prevailed in national politics and was most spectacularly evidenced when supporters first of Calhoun, then of Jackson, sought to evade the state and congressional caucuses in 1823 and 1824 by inventing the device of party conventions. Indeed, recourse to extraconstitutionality is a never-ending theme of American politics.

25 *Acts, 1792*, 1st sess., chap. 4, sec. 4; Frank F. Mathias, "The Turbulent Years of Kentucky Politics, 1820–1850" (Ph.D. diss., Univ. of Ky., 1966), pp. 7–12; *Acts, 1841–1842*, chap. 377, sec. 14; *Commonwealth*, 1, 8, 15 August 1843.

Political behavior at the county court level also demonstrates the continual fruitful interaction which exists between men and the constitutional system created by them. Men certainly interpret Constitutions; conversely, Constitutions influence men. While the county political leaders of Kentucky sought to alter in meaningful ways the formal structure of county government by petitions, meetings, rump sessions, and informal elections, they were nonetheless bound by the formal constitutional framework in which they operated. County politicians were therefore oligarchs largely because the state Constitution required them to be.

All this suggests that the county court system in Kentucky was ripe for constitutional change. After 1827 it produced far too many frustrated citizens to survive for any length of time. Every county party leader who could win at the polls but could not influence his own local government became an enemy of the system. So too did the thousands of county residents who found their districts without magistrates because of deliberate regional proscription. Inequities in the form and practice of politics at the county level contributed a powerful impulse for constitutional reform of the old county court system.

Chapter 5

COUNTY COURT PATRONAGE

THE POLITICAL BATTLES of local government in ante-bellum Kentucky were not waged exclusively over control of the county courts themselves. Politicians also regularly warred over the dispensation of county court patronage. Under the Constitution of 1799 the court appointed virtually every officer of the county: clerk, constables, jailer, coroner, surveyor, sheriff, and county attorney, all of whom served for life except the latter two, who served for two- and one-year terms respectively, and the jailer, who served at the pleasure of the court. Most of the conflict concerned the office of sheriff, the most powerful position in the county. Financially the office offered rewards in the form of commissions for collecting county and state taxes and fees for executing the orders of various courts—circuit, county, or military. Politically the office held official and unofficial power. In a formal sense the sheriff had potential influence since he was chief election officer of the county; not infrequently sheriffs became embroiled in local election disputes, and charges of fraud were not uncommon. Informally the sheriff maintained even greater political leverage by virtue of his position as chief executive officer of the local courts. Most sheriffs were active political partisans, and it was not unusual to see one of them drifting through the crowd at a polling place, his pockets filled with summonses and judgments which he would threaten to serve or execute upon wavering voters unless votes were cast for the "proper" candidates. Since during the period of the second Constitution voting was done by voice rather than by secret ballot, a strict accounting of campaign "promises" was entirely possible.

Although the relatively short-lived first Constitution provided for the election of sheriffs, the second Constitution gave the county courts a direct role in their selection. It provided that every two years each county court should meet and recommend to the governor two of its members for the sheriffalty, paying "a just regard to seniority in office and a regular rotation." If the court made a prompt recommendation, the governor was bound to commission one of the two magistrates selected; if not, he was empowered to fill the office with the advice and consent of the state Senate.

As the drafters of the Constitution foresaw, county courts not infrequently either failed completely to recommend magistrates for the sheriffalty or were dilatory. As a result an aura of extraconstitutionality grew up around appointments to this important office. While most omissions to recommend were attributable to lack of quorums or prolonged contests, some were deliberate. For example, the Breckinridge County Court declined to choose a nominee in 1821 because its senior justice of the peace was a convicted perjurer. Likewise the Lawrence County Court refused to make a recommendation in 1846 because its senior magistrate "too freely indulged in the use of ardent spirits" and was otherwise unstable. Sometimes the senior justice, obviously miffed at missing his opportunity for formal recommendation, solicited the sheriffalty directly from the governor, to whom the principal task of selection had fallen. At other times members of the court, apologetic for their neglect, offered to petition the governor in behalf of the senior magistrate. Occasionally a person (or persons) not associated with the county court solicited a commission from the governor and legislature; this was most likely to occur when the senior justice of the peace was in bad repute. There were also instances in which the governor reappointed an incumbent sheriff, especially when it was obvious that the county court hoped for such a result.[1]

Usually when county courts sent recommendations to the governor after the November deadline he chose to accept the nominee, even when the office was contested by groups not affiliated with the court. In early 1848 Governor Owsley commissioned John M. Austin sheriff of Butler County, although the court's recommendation of Austin was late and a third party, one N. Harreld, secretly sought the office. Owsley likewise commissioned Jonathan C. Langston sheriff of Caldwell County in June 1846, although his recommendation had been received seven months after the deadline.[2]

County court members also sought to influence appointments to fill vacancies in the sheriffalty resulting from death, resignation, or removal, even though by statute this privilege was reserved to the governor and the state Senate. At times courts claimed the power to furnish the governor with a binding recommendation, as in the case of the Adair County tribunal, which in late 1840 sought to secure the sheriffalty for the next magistrate in rotation after the senior member of the tribunal had refused the commission. This effort failed, for Governor Letcher appointed William

---

1 Copy of Breckinridge County Court Order, November term, 1821, Adair Papers, jacket 219 (G.P., reel 25). Z. Cushing to Governor William Owsley, 31 December 1846; James Richard and Isaac Botts to James M. Rice, 31 December 1846; James M. Rice to Owsley, 7 January 1847; and George F. Hatcher to Owsley, 22 February 1847, all in Owsley Papers, jacket 651 (G.P., reel 94).

2 John M. Austin to Governor William Owsley, 25 December 1847, Owsley Papers, jacket 704 (G.P., reel 98). Austin's commission is noted on the front of the letter. Copy of Caldwell County Court Order, June term, 1846, Owsley Papers, jacket 568 (G.P., reel 84).

G. Lobban, who was not a member of the court and who successfully challenged the right of the tribunal to dictate the governor's choice. In other instances, delegating their statutory duty, governors expressly left the decision up to county courts. Most often certain members of local tribunals sought to act informally by sending to governors petitions purporting not to be binding recommendations but mere suggestions. Thus in July 1833 three members of the Christian County Court wrote to Governor John Breathitt that they had heard that the present sheriff would soon resign and presented John Buckner as a "suitable person to fill the vacancy." [3]

One of the most controversial aspects of this appointment process concerned the constitutional provision obliging courts to "pay a just regard to seniority in office and a regular rotation." For many years it was supposed that this clause required the county courts to nominate the two magistrates ranking highest in seniority, and any failure to do so aroused quick protest. In certain instances county courts deliberately passed over senior magistrates, sometimes on the pretense that they were unfit for the sheriffalty. This happened in Franklin County early in the nineteenth century when the county court refused to recommend Henry Bartlett for the office, even though he maintained that he was the senior magistrate. Bartlett had earlier secured a writ of *mandamus* from the Court of Appeals temporarily restraining the county court from removing him from office on the grounds of insanity. When the court failed to recommend him, he appealed directly to the governor and eventually was commissioned. The tradition of recommending senior magistrates was so entrenched in the state's constitu-

3 Z. Wheat to Governor Robert Letcher, 7 December 1840, Letcher Papers, jacket 390 (G.P., reel 56). C. Sakin, A. Wilson, and Linah Minz to Governor John Breathitt, 12 July 1833, Breathitt Papers, jacket 325 (G.P., reel 37).

tional practice that in late 1829 when the Monroe County Court failed to adhere to this custom, Governor Thomas Metcalfe ignored the tribunal's nominee and nominated the senior justice of the peace to be sheriff. The Senate overwhelmingly endorsed Metcalfe's action.[4]

The custom of seniority also produced disputes over which member of a court had served the longest. By statute the magistrate who had first been commissioned ranked highest in seniority, but the county records did not always make this clear.[5] Usually county courts attempted to resolve disagreements by making a recommendation to the governor. The man who ranked second in the recommendation sometimes then appealed to the governor, but he seldom overturned the decision of the county court. On occasion courts were evenly divided over whom to recommend, forcing the governor to solve the dilemma in a *de novo* capacity.

Several events occurred during the later decades of the old county court system which served partially to undermine the assumption that only senior magistrates could be recommended for the sheriffalty. In 1833 Governor Breathitt in effect ruled that a senior justice of the peace who had been commissioned sheriff could waive his right to the office by failing to qualify. In 1831 the senior magistrate of Campbell County, William Anderson, was commissioned sheriff after being duly recommended by the county court but was unable to furnish security and therefore did not take the

[4] Henry Bartlett to Governor James Garrard, 15 April 1803, Garrard Papers, jacket 29 (G.P., reel 5); Franklin County Court Order Book, 1801–1805, pp. 175, 219 (U.K. microfilm, reel M:430:1486–87); *S.J., 1829–1830*, pp. 132–34. Soon after the second Constitution went into effect, John Snoddy complained to Joseph Hamilton Daveiss that the Madison County Court had failed to appoint him sheriff even though he was the senior justice of the peace and requested Daveiss "to take such steps and measures as your good Judgment may direct agreeable to the laws of our County" to force the magistrates to live up to their duties. Snoddy to Daveiss, 30 October 1800. Daveiss Papers, AD 2551 (Filson Club, Louisville, Ky.).

[5] *Acts, 1801*, chap. 56, sec. 3.

oath of office. Two years later the Campbell County Court passed over Anderson for the sheriffalty, prompting him to appeal to Governor Breathitt for redress. Breathitt ruled that Anderson was not entitled to the office, presumably concluding that he had waived his right by failing to qualify two years before. Governor Owsley solidified this precedent in 1846 when he refused to commission as sheriff the senior magistrate of Jefferson County on the grounds that he had waived his right to that office some ten years earlier by consenting to be passed over by the county court, even though at that time he was first in seniority.[6]

In October 1840, O. G. Cates, state attorney general, rendered the most potentially damaging blow to the tradition of seniority by ruling that county courts could recommend any two justices of the peace to be sheriff regardless of length of service. Such seemed to Cates to "have been the intention, spirit and meaning of the constitution." He believed that any other policy could result in the recommendation of senior magistrates who might be incapacitated by "mental imbecility or moral depravity."[7] Cates's opinion appears not to have found much currency during the remaining eleven years of the old county court system, perhaps because it was not well publicized. Magistrates continued to argue over who had served the longest, and county courts continued to adhere to the slightly tarnished tradition of seniority.

Only rarely, as when the first choice was shown to be morally unsound or incompetent, did governors fail to com-

6 William Anderson's petition to Governor John Breathitt, n.d.; copy of Campbell County Court order respecting the sheriffalty, 25 November 1833; William Wright Southgate to Breathitt, 5 December 1833, all in Breathitt Papers, jacket 338 (G.P., reel 37); Owsley Papers, jacket 610 (G.P., reel 89).

7 O.G. Cates to James Harlan, 17 October 1840, Letcher Letter Book, pp. 2–5 (G.P., reel 54). Harlan, secretary of state, had asked Cates for his opinion on the validity of a recommendation of the Jefferson County Court which did not pay "just regard to seniority."

mission magistrates listed first in the recommendations of the courts. Thus in 1845 opponents of George W. Kouns successfully blocked his nomination for the sheriffalty of Carter County on the grounds that he was under indictment for rape. Yet their victory was only temporary, for as soon as Kouns was cleared of rape charges and had barely survived an attempt by the General Assembly to remove him from office, the county court recommended him again for sheriff, and this time he was commissioned. In another instance Governor Charles Scott refused to commission either choice of the Pulaski County Court even though the two magistrates were the ranking members of the court. Scott defended his action by asserting that both candidates had disqualified themselves by being members of the legislature which had voted to increase the fees of the sheriffalty.[8]

Party politics does not seem to have influenced significantly patronage battles over the sheriff's office. In part this was because the method by which sheriffs were selected did not allow much opportunity for party manipulation. It was more crucial and rewarding for political parties to fight over control of county courts since they controlled the appointment of sheriffs. In addition, most recommendations were beyond contest. Only when senior magistrates were vulnerable on legal or moral grounds did out political groups intervene, and even in these cases the potential rewards were normally not great since the magistrates next in seniority were often members of the entrenched faction. Furthermore, it was usually easy for well-to-do politicians to become sheriffs by simply purchasing the office from its newly commissioned occupant.

The widespread practice of selling public offices in Kentucky doubtless accounts in large part for the absence of partisan political battles over the office of sheriff. It also

8 Owsley Papers, jackets 612, 651 (G.P., reels 84, 94); Charles Scott Journal, 17 December 1808 (G.P., reel 8).

helps explain why there appear to have been few patronage fights over other offices of the local constitution, such as deputy sheriff, county clerk, and the constable. Furthermore, the tradition of bargain and sale explains why party control of the county court did not always mean that all the patronage went to members of the same party, although frequently this was the case. In all the transactions involving the sale of county office, money, not political affiliation, was the paramount consideration. Thus, for example, a Whig could easily buy a sheriffalty in a county run by a Democratic court. This happened often in Fayette County, where, from 1833 to 1851, although there was always a preponderance of Democratic magistrates, half of the sheriffs and approximately half of the constables were Whigs. The Democratic justices of the peace, who presumably sold the offices, were more interested in profit than in politics.[9]

The system of rotation and seniority encouraged the farming or selling of the sheriffalty since by the time a justice of the peace reached a position of seniority on the court he was often too old and feeble to carry out the duties of office. These duties were onerous and, as one newspaper put it, unless the sheriff-designate was equipped "to be moving continually on horseback, or on foot, in all sorts of weather, over all sorts of roads, and sometimes at night, as well as during the day . . . he is unfit for the office." Many farmed or sold the office because they were unfit. For example, by the time Price Nuttall, a leading citizen and magistrate of Henry County, had served long enough to become sheriff, he was "quite an old man and in a very feeble state of health and apprehend[ed] that he [would]

---

[9] Because of the lack of evidence it is impossible to determine the party affiliations of all the constables of Fayette County from 1833 to 1851. Each party claimed the other had a majority. See, for example, the Democratic claim in the *Gazette*, 7 December 1844, and the Whig claim in the *Observer and Reporter*, 2 December 1844. From the available evidence it is estimated that each party "bought" its fair share, approximately one-half.

live but a short time." Upon being commissioned sheriff in 1843, he promptly sold the office to a deputy and resigned. Physical infirmity was not the only reason for selling the sheriffalty. Sometimes a newly commissioned sheriff or a senior magistrate sold his office or right thereto because he needed money. In early 1829 former United States Senator John Brown sold the office of sheriff of Franklin County even before he had received it to raise money for his son Orlando, a struggling young lawyer in Alabama. Custom also was a powerful stimulus to sell the office of sheriff. Indeed it was almost assumed that the senior justice of the peace in a large and prosperous county would sell the sheriffalty rather than serve in office so that he might reap immediately the financial reward for his long and generally unprofitable service on the county court.[10]

A newly appointed sheriff could sell all or part of his official responsibilities. He could sell his office, usually to a deputy, and resign, or he might simply refuse to post bond and thus not qualify. In either case he would have taken care to ensure that his vendee would be commissioned his successor by the governor. Apparently all that this required was a letter of resignation to the governor recommending the purchaser, although not naming him as such, as successor. If the sheriff-designate did not wish to abdicate his post entirely, he might farm all or part of it to one of his deputies. No matter if the office was sold, farmed out, or partially leased, those who did business with the sheriff had to idemnify him for losses he might suffer as a result of their conduct.

It was not uncommon for the sheriffalty to be auctioned off at a public sale. One critic accused senior magistrates of allowing "the office to be hawked about the streets, and sold

10 *Convention*, 20 February 1847; Thomas B. Posey to Governor Robert Letcher, 15 March 1843, Letcher Papers, jacket 469 (G.P., reel 70); John Brown to Orlando Brown, 17 March 1829, folder 4, Orlando Brown Papers (Filson Club, Louisville, Ky.).

like a horse in the public market, so that he who had the most money might get the office." One such auction took place in Jessamine County in January 1847 and another in Marion County only a few months earlier.[11]

Prices paid for farming or buying the sheriffalty varied from county to county. That of a populous and prosperous county would normally command a larger price since the amount of collectible taxes and hence the commission would be greater. Furthermore, there would be more litigation, more papers to serve, and more judgments to execute. The sheriffalty of Fayette County, second only to Jefferson in population and wealth, sold for around $2,000 per two-year term. In Jefferson County the office probably sold for twice that amount. In Jessamine County it was sold in the streets of Nicholasville, the county seat, for $1,000 in January 1847, while the price was $1,200 in Clark County some two years earlier. The sheriffalty of Montgomery County customarily brought from $1,000 to $1,200 per term. Estimations of the average price paid for a sheriffalty ranged from $500 to $800.[12]

It is difficult to determine how many sheriffalties were either sold or farmed during the fifty-one-year life of the second state Constitution. Certainly in some counties, such as Bourbon or Montgomery, where the economy was relatively prosperous, the office was nearly always sold by the senior justice of the peace upon receiving his commission. The competition was so intense in Bourbon County that the office was frequently sold one or two years in advance of the time in which the seller would receive his commission. A

11 Remarks of Beverly L. Clarke, delegate from Simpson County, at the Constitutional Convention of 1849, *Proceedings*, p. 387; *Convention*, 30 January 1847.

12 *Convention*, 30 January, 20 March, 17 July 1847; Report of the Special Committee on the Sale of Public Office, *H.J., 1845–1846*, pp. 338–39; speech of Francis M. Bristow, delegate from Todd County, at the Constitutional Convention of 1849, *Proceedings*, p. 715.

special committee established in January 1846 by the state House of Representatives to investigate the buying and selling of public office in Kentucky concluded that the sheriffalty was probably sold in nearly every county, but this determination was made after studying only one county in depth and seems exaggerated. In many of the poorer and more sparsely settled counties the sheriffalty seems not to have been solicited. J. C. Roundtree resigned as sheriff of Edmonson County in 1845, writing to a friend that the office was so worthless he could not even afford the services of a deputy. The fact that some county courts simply neglected to recommend magistrates for the sheriffalty suggests that the office was often not coveted. It is perhaps safest to surmise that the office of sheriff was frequently bought or farmed in those counties with strong economies and active court systems but was seldom the object of the governmental entrepreneur in the less wealthy counties.[13]

A senior justice of the peace who accepted a commission to the sheriffalty automatically vacated his magistracy and his place on the county court. Most who thereafter sold the sheriffalty retired permanently from county government, but a few sought reappointment to the county court, and some of these produced considerable controversy as well as interesting constitutional problems. In late 1842 John McKee as senior justice of the peace was commissioned sheriff of Franklin County. Soon afterward McKee sold his office and then secured the county court's recommendation to fill the seat he had vacated—a simple task since the McKee family controlled much of county government in Franklin. McKee's move elicited an outburst from the residents of the county, especially the Whigs, who had generally been pro-

[13] *Yeoman*, 21 January 1847; Report of the Special Committee, *H.J.*, *1845–1846*, pp. 338–39; J. C. Roundtree to W. John Burnam, 17 January 1845, Owsley Papers, jacket 568 (G.P., reel 84); Christopher Greenup Journal, 22 January 1808 (G.P., reel 8).

scribed from the court and who saw this effort at self-perpetuation as an opportunity to strike a blow at the entrenched opposition. Petitions poured into Governor Robert Letcher's office protesting the recommendation of McKee and promoting the court's second choice, Samuel B. Scofield, who lived in an area without a justice of the peace. Letcher was in a quandary; after deliberating for more than a week he wrote an eight-page letter to McKee denying him reappointment to the county court. He informed McKee that although it was his normal practice "to confer the appointment upon the person first named in the order of recommendation" and while he believed that McKee was well qualified to be a magistrate, on this occasion he was appointing the court's second choice to avoid a possible violation of the Constitution. To do otherwise, he argued, would be to allow McKee to serve as justice of the peace while enjoying the profits of an incompatible office, the sheriffalty. The court, Letcher concluded, would be converted "with its self-perpetuating power" into "an ever-lasting power." [14]

In contrast to such spirited battles over the sheriffalty, political entrepreneurs seldom, if ever, fought over the deputy sheriff's office. Aspirants usually confined their politicking, if any was needed, to the support of individual candidates for sheriff since the sheriff appointed his own deputies with the approval of the county court. Such an occasion presented itself in Washington County in 1846. Two justices of the peace, one a Democrat and the other a Whig, sought the office of sheriff, both claiming to be the senior magistrate. The Democrat received the active support of two Whig constables by promising to name them as his deputies. This show of strength, added to a slim Jack-

14 John McKee to Governor Robert Letcher, 17 July 1843, and six petitions to Letcher, Letcher Papers, jacket 482 (G.P., reel 73); Letcher to McKee, 28 August 1843, Letcher Papers, jacket 466 (G.P., reel 70).

sonian majority on the court, prompted endorsement of the Democrat ahead of the Whig, and the governor acceded to this recommendation.[15]

The role of the county court in the appointment of deputy sheriffs was limited both because it merely approved the nominations of the high sheriff and because these offices were inevitably the objects of agreements to purchase or farm part of the total profits of the sheriffalty. Normally a sheriff sold deputyships to the highest bidder, and unlike those for the sheriffalty, the transactions for deputyships seem always to have been carried on in private. In some instances groups purchased a deputyship, and although the duties of the office would be carried out by only one of the buyers, the profits would be divided among them. There appears to have been a tendency on the part of certain senior justices of the peace who executed the office of sheriff themselves to sell deputyships to their former constables, the executive officers of the magistrates.[16]

Although the county courts were empowered by the Constitution to appoint their own clerks, they appear in practice to have shared this task with outgoing clerks and, in many cases, judges of the circuit courts, as a part of transactions of bargain and sale. Many clerkships of both the county and circuit courts were sold, often to the same man. Since both the members of the county court and the judge of the circuit court were given the exclusive right to name their own clerks, presumably the justices and judges either delegated their responsibilities to outgoing clerks for a

15 (Unknown) to Governor William Owsley, 28 October 1846, and Richard Brown to Owsley, 26 October 1846, Owsley Papers, jacket 611 (G.P., reel 89).

16 *Yeoman*, 8 October 1846; *Convention*, 20 February 1847; Report of the Special Committee, *H.J., 1845–1846*, pp. 338–39; Richard Brown to Governor William Owsley, 26 October 1846; (Unknown) to Owsley, 28 October 1846, Owsley Papers, jacket 611 (G.P., reel 89).

share of the profits of the sale or sold the office themselves
when the incumbent had died or had been involuntarily
removed from his position.

County clerkships were more offices of profit than of political power, although on occasion clerks were able to aid
entrenched political groups.[17] Sometimes a transaction concerning the clerkship involved leasing as well as selling, as
in the case of John D. Young, clerk of the Fayette County
Court, who in 1816 farmed his office to Abner Fields for one
year, receiving $1,000 for the lease. Before the end of the
period of the lease, Young sold the office to James C. Rodes
for $6,000. Rodes thereupon paid Fields $400 in the form of
eight $50 notes in return for the latter's promise to execute
all the clerk's business until the expiration of Fields's one-
year lease. On other occasions the clerkship was simply
leased, as evidenced by the statement of one Newton P.
Reed before a committee of the state House of Representatives in 1846. Reed testified that the clerkship of the Montgomery County Court had recently been leased at $250 per
year for a period of four years.[18]

Of the remaining county offices which were filled by the
county court, only the constabulary appears to have been
sold during the antebellum period, although it would have
been quite natural for others, such as the coroner's office

[17] The duties of the clerk of the county court included the recording of
various legal documents such as deeds and wills, the selling of various licenses including those to operate billiard tables and sell watches, and the
keeping of the county court order book. For most of his services the clerk
received fees, the abundance of which made the office one of substantial
profit. On occasion clerks intervened in political warfare, as in 1844 when
the clerk of the Morgan County Court refused to copy an order of the court
to expedite a frustrated office seeker's petition to the governor. William
Ragland to Governor William Owsley, 23 November 1844, Owsley Papers,
jacket 568 (G.P., reel 84).

[18] *Outon v. Rodes*, 3 A. K. Marshall 432 (1821); *Commonwealth v. Rodes*,
1 Dana 595 (1833); Report of the Special Committee, *H.J., 1845–1846*, pp.
338–39.

and the jailer's office, to have been the object of private
bidding. Perhaps the relative insignificance of the latter
positions explains why there is no evidence that they were
sold or farmed. The constabulary, however, was an office
not only of some profit but of political power as well. Constables were the executive officers of justices of the peace
serving their summonses and other papers and carrying out
their orders and judgments. Although constables had no
formal political functions such as overseeing elections, they
unofficially exercised influence on election day in much the
same way the sheriff did, by waving summonses and unexecuted judgments in the faces of voters to coerce them to support a certain candidate.[19] Thus the political and appointive
nature of this office made it attractive for sale. Although very
little data is available on the mechanics of such transactions,
constableships were apparently sold by individual justices
of the peace or groups of them to the ever-present governmental enterpreneurs for prices as high as $400.

Legislators, judges, and prosecutors responded to these
practices inconsistently and ineffectively. The General Assembly prohibited the buying of office in 1801; yet in 1820
it declared bonds of indemnity binding even when executed
in consideration of a sale of a deputyship. Between 1817
and 1822 the Court of Appeals, in three civil actions, voided
two such bonds and held a lease of a county clerkship
invalid, but seemingly reversed itself in 1829 when it upheld a bond issued to indemnify the vendor of a deputy
sheriffalty. For the most part prosecutors did not prosecute,
and the first indictment against a buyer of office was not issued until 1843.[20]

19 Remarks of Elijah F. Nuttall, delegate from Henry County, at the
Constitutional Convention of 1849, *Proceedings*, p. 385.

20 *Acts, 1801*, chap. 57, sec. 29; *Acts, 1820*, chap. 149; *Love* v. *Buckner*, 4
Bibb 506 (1817); *Davis* v. *Hull*, 1 Littell 9 (1822); *Outon* v. *Rodes*, 3 A. K.
Marshall 432 (1821); *Baldwin* v. *Bridges*, 2 J. J. Marshall 7 (1829); Charles

The acquiescence and in many cases participation of the county courts in the selling and leasing of county offices not only were often products of corruption but tended to generate and perpetuate further corruption and incompetence. The buying and farming of the sheriffalty led to many other abuses and generally degraded the office from its already low status in 1800. Naturally a buyer of the office was eager to make as much profit as possible from his venture; frequently he extracted all possible fees and engaged in the corrupt practice of "shaving," that is, accepting a portion of a judgment in return for executing it. In addition to these harsh and illegal practices, selling or farming often produced incompetent sheriffs. So inept was the deputy sheriff of Hickman County, who had farmed the office from the sheriff, that Thomas James, a leading Democratic politician of the county, felt compelled to denounce him even though he was a fellow party member. James accused the deputy of being insolvent, corrupt, and a leader of lawless mobs assembled "for the purpose of putting down the civil authorities." [21]

As in the case of the sheriffalty, the sale of clerkships, deputy sheriffalties, and constableships contributed to abuses. Clerks were wont to extract as much revenue as possible from their investment even if it meant further corruption. James C. Rodes, who bought the clerkship of Fayette County in 1816 for $6,000, was acquitted of charges of malfeasance in 1833 before being removed from office in 1845 for embezzlement, extortion, and fraud. Deputy sheriffs and constables not infrequently augmented their income by unlawful activities such as forcing creditors to

---

G. C. Wintersmith to Governor Robert Letcher, 21 May 1843, Letcher Papers, jacket 468 (G.P., reel 70).

[21] Thomas James to Governor William Owsley, 7 March 1845, Owsley Papers, jacket 508 (G.P., reel 77).

share the proceeds of an executed judgment or simply purchasing a judgment at a discounted price, then executing it at its face value.[22]

Ultimately the collusion of county courts in these venal practices prompted efforts at reform. At first specific attempts, all unsuccessful, were made to enact more effective statutes outlawing the selling or farming of office. Governor Gabriel Slaughter recommended the passage of such a law in his annual message of 1816. When a bill outlawing the sale of office was finally introduced into the legislature in 1832 the Senate rejected it. In the following decade reformers turned their efforts away from measures aimed specifically at abolishing the sale of public office and instead cited the practice as only one reason to alter the entire structure of county government. In 1846 a group of seventy-eight Whig and Democratic legislators issued a call for a constitutional convention, citing the sale of public office as a primary cause for their action. The courts' powers of self-perpetuation and the widespread practice of selling the offices of the court contributed significantly to growing public disenchantment over county government.[23]

Problems and political struggles resulted not only from efforts to gain offices but also from attempts by county courts to remove officers. By statutory provision the county courts were empowered to remove for cause the jailer and any of the constables and to declare vacant the offices of justice of the peace, surveyor, and sheriff and move to initiate the commissioning of replacements; they could also

22 *Commonwealth* v. *Rodes*, 1 Dana 595 (1833); Fayette County Court Order Book, 1840–1846, pp. 513–14 (U.K. microfilm, reel M311:2031–32); Speech of James Guthrie, delegate from Louisville, at the Constitutional Convention of 1849, *Proceedings*, p. 374.

23 Message of Governor Gabriel Slaughter, 2 December 1816, *H.J.*, *1816–1817*, p. 18; *S.J.*, *1832–1833*, pp. 174–77; *Yeoman*, 8 October 1846.

block efforts by newly commissioned sheriffs to secure the appointment of certain men as their deputies.[24]

One of the most dramatic instances of removal occurred in 1845 in Franklin County. In its June term that year the Democratic county court sought to remove from office the Whig county jailer, William Gorham, precipitating a full-blown constitutional crisis involving conflicts with the Court of Appeals, the circuit court of the county, the General Assembly, and the Whig party, as well as the jailer himself. The political ambitions of certain members of the Franklin County Court underlay its decision to remove Gorham from office. Two justices of the peace, Benjamin Luckett and an unidentified magistrate, had applied for the office of deputy postmaster of Frankfort. Although Luckett possessed "a respectable recommendation for the office," his fellow magistrate was the choice of the Democratic State Central Committee. Furthermore, Luckett was the third senior member of the county court and as such would soon be entitled to the sheriffalty. Because of the need to remove him as a candidate for the deputy postmastership and because of the alleged desire on the part of some junior magistrates to advance up the ladder of succession to the sheriffalty, pressure was put upon Luckett to resign from the county court and accept the office of jailer. Luckett agreed to this, but probably not without some misgivings since the position of jailer was rather insignificant, especially when contrasted with that of sheriff, which was selling for approximately $1,300 a term. It may well be that his Democratic rivals on the court promised to give Luckett a percentage of the proceeds when they sold the office of sheriff in return for his promise to resign. The scheming magistrates of Franklin County also approached Gorham in private and urged him to resign to make way for Luckett,

---

24 *Acts, 1802*, chap. 53, sec. 20 (jailer); *Acts, 1803*, chap. 1, sec. 6 (constables).

but he would not comply.[25] His obstinance did not deter
the conspirators, and on the first day of the June term, without any appearance of deliberation, they handed the clerk
of the court an order removing Gorham for unspecified
"divers good causes" and appointing Luckett, who had
shortly before resigned from the court, in his stead.[26]

Later in the day both Gorham and Luckett appeared in
court with their attorneys, Gorham's counsel to offer a
motion to set aside the court's order and Luckett's to argue
against this move. The gist of Gorham's argument was that
a proceeding to remove a county jailer was judicial, not
ministerial, and that he had to be formally charged and
tried to be removed from office. The court allowed Gorham's attorney to produce one witness, a member of the
court, who was said to have been involved in the conspiracy
of removal and who would prove that no charges had been
preferred against the jailer. This offer of proof must have
shocked the Democratic justices since apparently one of
their number was betraying them. But the court quickly re-
covered its composure and dismissed the witness midway in
his testimony, ostensibly on the grounds that as a member of
the court he was an incompetent witness, but in reality, according to a Whig observer, because the assembled magistrates feared the revelation of the "real motive of dismissal."
Having discharged the witness, the court dismissed Gorham's motion, prompting the aggrieved jailer to obtain a
writ of error from the Court of Appeals.

On the following day the Democratic majority of the
court revealed that it was not altogether confident of the
legality of its decision in the Gorham case by striking out
the entry in its order book accepting the resignation of

25 The best review of the political aspirations underlying the Franklin
County jailer dispute is in the *Commonwealth*, 23 June 1846.

26 Franklin County Court Order Book, 1839–1848, p. 262 (U.K. microfilm,
reel M430:1488–89).

Luckett as justice of the peace. However, the Democratic magistrates apparently regained their confidence by November 1845, when they chose to defy an order of the Court of Appeals invalidating the attempted removal of Gorham as jailer. Gorham's counsel had convinced the high court in October that a proceeding to remove a jailer was judicial in nature and that the actions of the Franklin County Court violated due process. He appeared before the county court at its November term, filed the mandate of the Court of Appeals with the cooperative clerk, a Whig, and then moved that the magistrates obey the decree by returning the jailer's keys to his client. The court not only overruled the motion, the only two Whig magistrates dissenting, but entered a lengthy defense of its defiance in the order book. In their manifesto the justices argued that the Court of Appeals had usurped the "power confided by the constitution of the state to the county court relative to the office of Jailer" and had acted illegally in decreeing that Gorham be restored to office. The magistrates felt dutybound to resist this "intermeddling" and "declare[d] to the world" that they would not abide by the ruling of the higher court. In short, the Democratic justices of the peace of Franklin County were nullifying the decision of the Court of Appeals.[27]

Predictably the Whigs of Franklin County denounced the county court's intransigence. The Whig newspaper of the county, the Frankfort *Commonwealth*, which had earlier applauded the opinion of the Court of Appeals and printed it in full, accused the Democratic magistrates of attempting "a civil revolution." The Democrats defended the court's action. The Democratic newspaper of the county, the *Kentucky Yeoman*, proposed that there was a higher law than that which emanated from the Court of Appeals and that

27 Ibid., pp. 267, 290–97; *Gorham* v. *Luckett,* 6 B. Monroe 146 (1845).

the Franklin County magistrates had acted in the name of that law, which was grounded in "the people."[28]

Meanwhile, both the Whig party and Gorham's attorney were busy trying to force the Franklin County Court to yield to the Court of Appeals. In January 1846 the Whigs introduced a bill in the legislature outlawing the usurpation of a public office in defiance of a decree from a court of competent jurisdiction and enacted the proposal into law after successfully warding off Democratic efforts to make the act inapplicable to the controversy in Franklin County.[29] In May 1846 Gorham's lawyer obtained a summons from the Court of Appeals requiring the justices of the peace of Franklin to appear at the June term to show cause why they should not be held in contempt of court.[30]

Still Luckett and his cohorts refused to submit. No actions were brought against them under the newly enacted state law which made their conduct theoretically criminal. When Gorham successfully brought an action of trespass against his rival jailer in the Franklin County Circuit Court, Luckett refused to comply with the court's decree and give up the keys to the jail which he was occupying unlawfully. A short time later six of the Democratic justices of the peace—rather than accede to the summons of the Court of Appeals, which had indicated informally that it was in a conciliatory mood—subjected themselves to incarceration in Benjamin Luckett's jail. There they resided for four days; then on June 20 they held magistrate's court for one another and reciprocally issued writs of *habeas corpus* requiring their ally, Luckett, to show cause for holding them

[28] The charges and countercharges are in the *Commonwealth*, 25 November 1845.

[29] *Acts, 1845–1846*, chap. 133. There is a clear party breakdown in all the relevant votes on the bill in both houses of the General Assembly. *S.J., 1845–1846*, pp. 93, 95, 159–60; *H.J., 1845–1846*, pp. 246–47.

[30] *Commonwealth*, 5 May 1846.

prisoners. When he answered that they were being held because they had violated a decree from the Court of Appeals,
they ruled that his response was inadequate and ordered
themselves released. The Whiggish Lexington *Observer
and Reporter* commented that the resistance seemed ever-
lasting.[31]

Finally, on or about June 27, the Jacksonian magistrates
announced through counsel and in a written pledge that
they would consent to the mandate of the Court of Appeals.
At the July term of the court the surrender seemed complete when the court voted to enter the decree and then
set aside the order removing Gorham and appointing Luckett. Yet this appearance of abdication was short-lived, for
the very next item of business concerned the receipt of a
letter from William A. Gorham resigning from the office
of jailer of Franklin County. Needless to say, the court accepted the resignation and almost immediately thereafter
appointed Luckett jailer. There is no evidence of why Gorham resigned. Possibly he believed that it was the only way
he could obtain an admission from his magisterial oppres-
sors that they had in theory been wrong when they had
removed him without just cause one year before. So ended
the attempt of the Franklin County Court to nullify a decree of the Court of Appeals.[32]

The Gorham incident not only reveals the realities of
the politics of county government in antebellum Kentucky
but also demonstrates the sometimes vitriolic relationships
between the county courts and various county officials,
higher courts, and the state legislature. It also suggests the
immense power of the county courts. The Franklin magistrates successfully defied the authority of a circuit court,

31 Ibid., 23 June 1846; *Observer and Reporter,* 27 June 1846.
32 *Commonwealth,* 30 June 1846; Franklin County Court Order Book,
1839–1848, pp. 325–26 (U.K. microfilm, reel M430:1488–89).

the Court of Appeals, and the General Assembly. Some of them made a farce out of a mandate of the highest judicial tribunal of the state. It appears that they yielded very little when they agreed to enter the decree of the Court of Appeals since at the same time they secured what they had desired all along, the resignation of the Whig jailer. At no time during the episode did the countervailing constitutional forces of the state—the jailer, the circuit court, the Court of Appeals, the legislature, or, implicitly, the commonwealth's attorney and the grand jury for Franklin County, who were equipped with a new statute making Luckett's obstinence a crime—appear able to deter nullification.

Other county officers more successfully resisted attempts of county courts to remove them. One of the most prolonged conflicts was between the court and the surveyor of Perry County. The magistrates attempted to remove the surveyor, John Duff, in August 1843 for failure to post a bond to secure the performance of the duties of his office. Duff refused to vacate his office and appealed for redress both to the governor and to the Perry County Circuit Court. In a letter to Governor Letcher, Duff asserted that he had been the victim of a "violent and unconstitutional proceeding of the county court" and of the malfeasance of the county clerk, who had refused to record the execution of his bond. Despite his allegations, the governor denied Duff's plea for relief. The surveyor then took his case to the circuit court where, after a delay of almost three years, the judge ruled for the county court. Despite these adverse developments, Duff refused to vacate his office. His conduct became so obnoxious that in October 1846, one month after the action of the circuit court, the bar of Perry County assembled to endorse Circuit Judge William B. Kinkead's opinion upholding the county court and requested that a copy of the decision be furnished for publication. Yet Duff remained in

office for another year and a half and resigned only after the
legislature impeached him and found him guilty of misconduct in office.[33]

Not all county officials who were subjected to removal
proceedings by county courts were as tenacious as William
Gorham and John Duff. In December 1811 the County
Court of Bourbon charged Thomas J. Glass with certain
malfeasances and sought to remove him from his constableship. Glass allegedly had extracted bribes from would-be
defendants in return for promises not to serve warrants,
had sold a debtor's property prior to an advertised public
sale, and had served an unexecuted warrant in order to obtain a fee. Rather than face trial on these counts, Glass
resigned in early January 1812.[34]

Although they were not empowered to remove their fellow members, county courts could declare seats vacant
and move to fill them by nominating two candidates to the
governor. This proceeding frequently occurred, especially
during the early years of the county court system when
Kentuckians were highly mobile and not a few justices of
the peace, without notice, moved out of the county or even
the state. Sometimes a justice of the peace left his county
only temporarily, but when he returned to take his seat on
the court, found it occupied by a new appointee. In 1801
George Elliott, a member of the Garrard County Court, took
his wife to Lexington for medical treatment and remained
there for several months. When Elliott returned to Garrard
in May 1801 and attempted to take his place on the county
court, he was denied his seat on the pretense that he had
vacated it. Rather than appeal to a court for redress, Elliott

33 John A. Duff to Governor Robert Letcher, 17 September 1843, Letcher
Papers, jacket 466 (G.P., reel 70); *Commonwealth*, 17 November 1846; *H.J.*,
1847–1848, p. 371; *Convention*, 22 February 1848.

34 Bourbon County Court Order Book, 1808–1812, pp. 452, 464, 468 (U.K.
microfilm, reel M277:1738–39).

petitioned the legislature to pass a special law restoring his place on the court. Elliott was apparently able to work out a settlement with the county court before the assembly considered his petition, for he was recorded as sitting on the tribunal in April 1802.[35]

County courts did not declare vacancies solely because of unannounced withdrawals from the county. In 1844 the Spencer County Court declared Alexander Harcourt's seat vacant because he had accepted the postmastership of Mount Eden, a position which was, by express constitutional provision, incompatible with any state or county office. Harcourt obtained a writ of *mandamus* from the Spencer Circuit Court ordering his seat on the county court restored on the grounds that the justices had sought to remove him and thereby to exercise a power reserved exclusively to the legislature and the governor. The Court of Appeals upheld the county court's action by dismissing the circuit court's writ. While recognizing that the county court had no power of removal, the Court of Appeals endorsed its action in this case by asserting that Harcourt had no standing to secure a writ of *mandamus* since he could not demonstrate that he was in law a justice of the peace, having accepted an incompatible office.[36]

Sometimes county courts declared the office of sheriff vacant because its newly appointed occupant failed to post bond securing the performance of official acts. Normally those who failed to furnish security were sincere in their desire to vacate office, but occasionally sheriffs did not desire to forfeit their responsibilities and resisted the county court when it attempted to nominate a new candidate. In 1847 the Bullitt County Court declared the sheriffalty vacant after James Samuel, newly appointed to that office, failed to

[35] *H.J., 1801*, pp. 61–62; Garrard County Court Order Book, 1797–1808, p. 240 (U.K. microfilm, reel M24:1939–40).
[36] *Justices of Spencer County v. Harcourt*, 4 B. Monroe 499 (1844).

execute bond as the county tax collector. Since the statutory period for nominations had passed, the county court simply recommended that Thomas J. Joice be nominated by the governor to the Senate as Samuel's replacement. Samuel, pleading imminent financial embarrassment, resisted the county court's action and succeeded in blocking the governor's nomination in the Senate, which rejected the notion that Samuel had vacated his post.[37] Samuel died soon thereafter, rendering moot the constitutional question.

County courts also retained the power to reject appointments of certain county officials. In 1842 the court of Fleming County refused to administer the oath of office to William S. Emmons, one of the sheriff's duly appointed deputies. The magistrates grounded their refusal on the fact that they had removed Emmons from a constableship only four years earlier because of malfeasance in office. Both the Fleming County Circuit Court and the Court of Appeals upheld the county court's decision, the high tribunal averring that the magistrates had "some discretion in guarding the public against a glaring and reckless abuse of power."[38]

The patronage battles of Franklin and Perry counties, although uniquely spectacular and protracted, helped to undermine public confidence in Kentucky's local government. The clumsiness which pervaded many of the more routine incidents of removal also contributed to the deteriorating posture of the county courts. By the mid-1840s reformers were seriously considering alternative ways to select and reject county officers.

37 *S.J., 1846–1847*, pp. 301, 373, 401–2, 427; *Commonwealth*, 16 March 1847.
38 *Day v. Justices of the Fleming County Court*, 3 B. Monroe 198 (1842).

Chapter 6

THE COUNTY COURTS
AND THE LEGISLATURE

THE COUNTY COURTS were not only the nucleus of
local government but also a major agent of state
government. In addition to such perennial tasks
as maintaining roads and collecting taxes, the courts performed special missions for the state such as procuring and
surveying land for seminaries of learning. Indeed the courts
almost always acted as agents of the state.

Almost all the powers of the county courts were legislatively granted, for although they were of constitutional
origin during most of the antebellum period, their jurisdiction was dependent upon the General Assembly.
Their powers seemed to increase steadily as the legislators
delegated more and more responsibility to their "county
agents." The initial statute concerning county courts merely granted to them the power to hear "all cases respecting
wills, letters of administration, mills, roads, the appointment of guardians and settling of their accounts and the
admitting of deeds and other writings to record." [1] Thereafter the assembly added such powers as those to establish
uniform weights and measures, franchise ferries, license
sundry businesses, and establish gates and passways, while
it expanded other responsibilities.

So extensive were the responsibilities of the courts that
even their supporters began to denounce the legislature for

delegating so much of its authority to them. During the debates in 1837–1838 on the desirability of amending the state Constitution, Robert Nelson Wickliffe, a Lexington attorney and editor of the *Observer and Reporter*, accused the assembly of having "heaped upon the county court powers and required them to perform duties, in the exercise of which they became odious." R. D. Letcher of Garrard County asserted that "the inordinate power of the county court [was] given not by the Constitution but by the Legislature which had made it what it is."[2]

Not only did the legislature continuously expand the authority of the county courts, but it repeatedly overlooked and even ratified their abuses. Between 1808 and 1828, for example, the General Assembly enacted nineteen statutes either ratifying or permitting delinquent levies, eight statutes either ratifying or permitting delinquent appointments of tax commissioners, seven statutes ratifying the business of courts held on the wrong days, one statute permitting an extra session of a court, and ten miscellaneous acts either ratifying or permitting acts of dubious legality or of an extraordinary nature.

Yet the legislature was not altogether the compliant defender of the county court system. It did not always endorse dubious or extraconstitutional actions by the courts; outraged citizens petitioned it to overturn controversial orders of their county tribunals. The General Assembly passed a law in 1820 rescinding an order of the Greenup County Court establishing a two-dollar levy per tithable to appropriate funds for a county jail. On the other hand, the legislators often resisted efforts to annul the actions of local tribunals. For example, in 1809 they rejected a petition of a group of Clark County citizens to set aside an order of the county court to lay a levy for the building of a jail, and in

1 *Acts, 1792*, 1st sess., chap. 35, sec. 4.
2 *Gazette*, 18 January 1838; *Intelligencer*, 25 July 1838.

1816 they denied redress to petitioners from Allen County seeking the voidance of contracts for the construction of certain public buildings.[3]

Deepening the relationship of the legislature to the county courts were its continuous and usually unsuccessful attempts to regulate more effectively the proceedings of the tribunals and the conduct of various county officials, including the justices of the peace. The assembly made repeated efforts to increase the jurisdiction of the county courts and magistrates. Indeed it was always dealing with county government in one way or another.[4]

Since justices of the county courts were eligible for membership in the General Assembly, they were at least theoretically in a position to influence strongly the proceedings of the legislature, especially those concerning county government. Substantial numbers of them took advantage of their opportunity to serve in the state legislature. Records for most of the fifty-nine years from 1792 to 1851 indicate that nearly a fourth of the total membership of the House of Representatives and slightly less than a fifth of the Senate were acting county court justices.[5] Generally speaking, the number of justices of the peace serving in the House was

3 *Acts, 1820*, chap. 168; *H.J., 1808–1809*, p. 166; *H.J., 1815–1816*, pp. 123–24 (petition never reported out of committee).

4 During its session of 1840–1841 alone the House of Representatives considered well over seventy-five bills dealing with county courts. *H.J., 1840–1841*, Index, pp. 14–16.

5 See Table 1. Justices of the peace who served on the courts of quarter sessions and were in the legislature are not included in this list since they were not members of the county courts. Lists of legislators can be found in Lewis Collins and Richard H. Collins, *History of Kentucky*, 2 vols. (Covington, Ky., 1874), vol. 2, passim, *H.J., 1792–1851* and *S.J., 1792–1851* and the Frankfort *Palladium*; names of magistrates are located in the Journals and Papers of the Governors of Kentucky, 1792–1850, Registers of the Justices of the Peace, 1815–1820, 1835–1844, and 1845–1850 (G.P.), and county court order books. For the years not covered by the Registers, statistics are estimates since governors' journals and papers do not always indicate termination of magisterial tenure and not all county court order books are extant.

TABLE 1

COUNTY COURT MAGISTRATES IN THE LEGISLATURE
1792–1851

YEAR IN WHICH SESSION BEGAN	HOUSE MAGISTRATES	TOTAL HOUSE MEMBERSHIP	SENATE MAGISTRATES	TOTAL SENATE MEMBERSHIP
1792 (2d sess.)	15	40	2	11
1793	14	40	1	11
1794	17	42	2	11
1795	17	42	2	11
1796	26	56	evidence incomplete	evidence incomplete
1797	evidence incomplete	evidence incomplete	evidence incomplete	
1798 (7th ass.)	19	56	6	15
1799	25	58	evidence incomplete	evidence incomplete
Subtotal (1792–1799)	133 (39.8%)	334	13 (22%)	59
1800	17	62	8	25
1801	14	62	6	25
1802	13	62	6	25
1803	evidence incomplete	evidence incomplete	evidence incomplete	
1804	17	63	8	25
1805	19	63	5	25
1806	25	63	6	25
1807	26	63	9	25
1808	22	70	7	28
1809	27	70	8	28
1810	23	70	9	28
1811	25	70	8	28

1812	26	80	6	31
1813	26	80	11	31
1814	25	80	10	31
1815	19	80	9	31
1816	31	91	8	34
Subtotal (1800–1816)	355 (31.4%)	1129	124 (27.9%)	445
1817	16	91	6	34
1818	19	91	8	34
1819	22	91	4	34
1820	29	100	5	38
1821	24	100	9	38
1822	22	100	10	38
1823	18	100	13	38
1824	24	100	11	38
1825	29	100	7	38
1826	24	100	5	38
1827	25	100	5	38
1828	27	100	6	38
1829	18	100	9	38
1830	32	100	8	38
1831	25	100	8	38
1832	24	100	10	38
1833	23	100	8	38
1834	23	100	9	38
1835	26	100	7	38
Subtotal (1817–1835)	450 (24.0%)	1873	148 (20.8%)	710

TABLE 1–*Continued*

YEAR IN WHICH SESSION BEGAN	HOUSE MAGISTRATES	TOTAL HOUSE MEMBERSHIP	SENATE MAGISTRATES	TOTAL SENATE MEMBERSHIP
1836	17	100	6	38
1837	12	100	5	38
1838	21	100	5	38
1839	22	100	5	38
1840	18	100	5	38
1841	16	100	3	38
1842	17	100	3	38
1843	16	100	4	38
1844	17	100	5	38
1845	13	100	3	38
1846	17	100	3	38
1847	16	100	3	38
1848	14	100	5	38
1849	15	100	5	38
1850	11	100	3	38
Subtotal (1836–1850)	242(16.1%)	1500	63(11.1%)	570
Totals (1792–1850)	1180(24.4%)	4836	348(19.5%)	1784

greatest during the early years of statehood and gradually but unevenly decreased as time passed. In the Senate the pattern is even more erratic, although there were proportionately more county court magistrates in this body during the first half of the period of the old county court system than in the last.

It is evident that for the fifty-nine-year period under study the percentage of magistrates in the lower house was moderately greater than in the Senate. What is not so clear is why this was so or why the relative numbers of county court justices in both houses declined during the last fifteen years of the system. One explanation is that public opposition to the county courts, which intensified after 1835, translated itself into votes against magistrates running for the legislature. Except for this tentative supposition the decline remains mysterious.

There is data to establish the party affiliation of the legislative magistrates. While a majority of the county court justices serving in the legislature were members of the dominant Whig party, a substantial minority were Democrats. Statistics reveal that from 1827 to 1851, the earliest period of an organized and documented two-party system in the state, nearly 58 percent of the House magistrates were Whig and slightly over 42 percent were Democratic, while the Senate was divided almost equally between the two major parties. Democrats were actually more numerous among the magistrates of the assembly than in the membership at large. Through the legislature of 1850–1851 only 37 percent of the general membership of the House and Senate were Democrats, which means that proportionately there were almost 13 percent more Democrats among the justices of the peace in the House and 32 percent more among those in the Senate.[6]

6 See Table 2. Lists of legislators and their party affiliations can be found in the following newspapers: *Reporter* (1827–1829, 1831); *Argus of the West-*

TABLE 2

PARTY AFFILIATION OF COUNTY COURT MAGISTRATES IN THE LEGISLATURE
1827–1850

YEAR IN WHICH ASSEMBLY BEGAN	HOUSE MAGISTRATES		TOTAL HOUSE		SENATE MAGISTRATES		TOTAL SENATE	
	Democrat	Whig*	Democrat	Whig	Democrat	Whig	Democrat	Whig
1827	12	13	45**	54	1	4	17	21
1828	13	14	data unavailable		2	4	data unavailable	
1829	8	10	37	63	3	6	13	25
1830	14	18	52	48	3	5	21	17
1831	9	16	44	56	3	5	data unavailable	
1832	11	13	40	60	4	6	16	22
1833	10**	12	40	60	6	2	20	18
1834	8	15	25	75	6	3	16**	21
1835	12	14	39	61	5	2	16	22
1836	11	6	42	58	4	2	14	24
1837	2	10	23	77	2	3	13	25
1838	6	15	35	65	2	3	16	22
1839	8**	13	39	61	2	3	16	22
1840	5	13	24	76	2	3	14	24

Year								
1841	6	10	23	77	1	2	9**	27
1842	8	9	43	57	1	2	10	28
1843	6	10	35**	64	2	2	12	26
1844	8**	8	35**	64	2	3	12	26
1845	6	7	38	62	2	1	14	24
1846	6	11	37	63	2	1	12	26
1847	8	8	41	59	2	1	11	27
1848	6	8	36	64	2	3	11	27
1849	7	8	42	58	3	2	12	26
1850	5	6	44	56	3	0	13	25
	195	267	859	1438	65	68	308	525
	(42.2%)	(57.8%)	(37.4%)	(62.6%)	(48.9%)	(51.1%)	(37%)	(63%)

* The term *Whig* is used to describe the pro-Adams and Clay party which existed from 1827 to 1834 as well as the Whig Party which began in 1834.

** Political affiliation of one or more legislators unknown.

It is not surprising that the presence of so many county court justices in the General Assembly, which dealt so extensively with county government, produced periodic spasms of opposition. Complaints were especially prevalent during the early decades of the county court system and during the years immediately preceding constitutional reform in 1849. In March 1794 a "Farmer," writing to the *Kentucky Gazette,* denounced the practice of allowing justices of the peace, whom he characterized as "petty tyrants," to serve as both "makers and judges of the law." William Henry echoed "Farmer's" sentiments in October 1794 and urged the defeat of all magistrates running for the General Assembly. Both pleas apparently fell on deaf ears because substantial numbers of magistrates were elected to the legislature in 1794 and 1795.[7]

Failing to defeat significant numbers of the justices at the polls, critics turned to the device of constitutional reform. "Cassius," writing to the *Gazette* in May 1798, accused Kentuckians of "surrendering" their rights to the county magistrates, whom he pictured as controlling the legislature, and called for constitutional reform of this alleged grievance.[8] Although a new constitution was produced in the following year, county magistrates were not prohibited from serving in the legislature, and criticism of the practice continued into the first two decades of the nineteenth century.

Humphrey Marshall was especially caustic in his complaints about the legislative magistrates. He accused them

---

ern *World* (1828, 1832); Russellville *Weekly Messenger* (1828); *Gazette* (1830, 1835–1838); Louisville *Daily Focus* (1831); *Commonwealth* (1833–1835, 1838–1850); and *Observer and Reporter* (1839).

[7] *Gazette,* 1, 8 March, 4 October 1794. In 1795 both houses resolved that justices of the courts of quarter sessions were ineligible for the legislature; yet in 1799 the House defeated a similar resolution. *H.J., 1795,* pp. 9–10; *S.J., 1795,* p. 7; *H.J., 1799,* p. 11.

[8] Ibid., 2 May 1798.

of imposing on Kentuckians in 1792 and 1805 substantial fee schedules for justices of the peace and generally of voting to increase the powers of single magistrates and county courts. Other critics agreed. "Rusticus," writing to the *Gazette* in 1806, charged the legislative magistrates with increasing the fees of both justices of the peace and sheriffs. One detractor unsuccessfully attacked the validity of an 1805 statute that enlarged the jurisdiction of single magistrates by alleging that the presence of so many justices in the legislature rendered the law invalid because it violated the separation of powers doctrine. Twice early in the nineteenth century unsuccessful attempts were made to prevent House magistrates from voting on their own fee bills, and in 1808 Governor Scott refused to appoint either of two recommended justices to the sheriffalty of Pulaski County because both had voted as legislators for a sheriffs' fee bill.[9]

Voting records suggest that in part the charges of these critics were correct. On occasion legislative magistrates protected their fee schedules, supporting increases and opposing reductions. They also resisted attempts to prohibit magistrates from voting on such matters. For example in 1805 they voted overwhelmingly against an attempt to prevent legislative justices from voting on a magisterial fee bill and then supported the legislation, although less substantially. In 1808 they resisted a similar attempt of prohibition and generally opposed an attempt to reduce their fees. Senate justices were equally on guard, voting, for example, six to one in 1819 against an attempt to lower rates.[10]

Yet this pattern is not uniform. In 1799 House magistrates voted fifteen to ten in favor of a key section of a bill substantially eliminating magisterial fees and in 1806 they

---

[9] Marshall, *History of Kentucky*, 2:33–37; *Gazette*, 19 July 1806; *Head v. Hughes*, 1 A. K. Marshall 372 (1818); *H.J., 1805*, pp. 92–93; *H.J., 1807–1808*, p. 129; Charles Scott Journal, p. 15 (G.P., reel 8).

[10] *H.J., 1805*, pp. 92–93; *H.J., 1807–1808*, pp. 129, 141; *S.J., 1818–1819*, p. 262.

voted eleven to ten to repeal in part the fee statute enacted the year before. Likewise, the assemblies of 1793 and 1798 lowered fees, and although votes were not recorded, the lower houses were heavily populated with justices of the peace. Recorded voting on other fee bills manifests significant division among the magistrates.[11]

With regard to bills enlarging the jurisdiction of single magistrates and county courts, critics of legislative justices clearly exaggerated both the extent and nature of the alleged conspiracy. In fact a majority of magistrates frequently voted against bills which would have extended the individual magistrates' powers or expanded the jurisdiction of their courts. In eighteen sample votes between 1792 and 1849 a majority of House justices voted thirteen times against bills which would have increased jurisdiction or for bills restricting jurisdiction, and in only four instances did they support increased jurisdiction; the remaining vote resulted in a tie. But in most cases a substantial minority of justices opposed the decision of the majority, undermining the notion that there existed a "magistrates' bloc" on this question. Although Senate magistrates were more apt to favor bills increasing jurisdiction of county government, they also on occasion evidenced substantial division on these questions.[12]

[11] *H.J., 1799*, p. 105; *H.J., 1806*, p. 59; Marshall, *History of Kentucky*, 2:33–37. For example, legislative magistrates divided almost equally on fee bills in 1809, 1810, 1811, and 1819. *H.J., 1808–1809*, pp. 262–64; *H.J., 1809–1810*, p. 187; *H.J., 1810–1811*, pp. 162–63; *H.J., 1819–1820*, p. 140.

[12] *H.J., 1792*, 2d sess., pp. 67–68; *H.J., 1801*, p. 96; *H.J., 1804*, p. 34; *H.J., 1805*, p. 97; *H.J., 1810–1811*, pp. 149–50; *H.J., 1815–1816*, p. 87; *H.J., 1821*, p. 269; *H.J., 1822*, p. 302; *H.J., 1826–1827*, pp. 30–31; *H.J., 1829–1830*, pp. 106–8; *H.J., 1838–1839*, pp. 554–55; *H.J., 1840–1841*, pp. 382–84; *H.J., 1841–1842*, pp. 209–12; *H.J., 1844–1845*, pp. 223–25; *H.J., 1845–1846*, pp. 109–10; *H.J., 1846–1847*, pp. 187–91; *H.J., 1847–1848*, pp. 183–85; *H.J., 1848–1849*, pp. 136–39. For examples of Senate voting see *S.J., 1805–1806*, p. 71; *S.J., 1810–1811*, pp. 184–85; *S.J., 1811–1812*, p. 156; *S.J., 1818–1819*, pp. 262–63; *S.J., 1819–1820*, pp. 160–61; *S.J., 1829–1830*, pp. 160–61; and *S.J., 1835–1836*, pp. 324–26.

Furthermore legislative magistrates were far from a self-conscious and powerful voting bloc when it came to two other categories of business affecting local government: attempts to remove errant justices of the peace and to regulate more effectively county government and its personnel. The General Assembly of Kentucky from time to time considered petitions calling for removal of one or more county court justices. The Constitutions of both 1792 and 1799 provided two methods to remove justices of the peace—impeachment by the House and conviction by the Senate, or an address to the governor approved by two-thirds of each house. The legislature normally utilized the latter method. The House dealt with most of these cases, the majority of which occurred before 1820. Nine of them afford some idea of how the legislative justices of the peace reacted when trying one of their brethren. In only two instances did a majority of magistrates in the House act decisively to prevent a fellow justice of the peace from being removed from office. In 1792 the House voted twenty-three to seven to reject a petition calling for the removal of John Waller, a magistrate and member of the court of quarter sessions of Bourbon County. The assembled justices of the peace voted six to one in Waller's favor. In 1810 the House voted thirty-six to nineteen to disapprove a recommendation from a select committee recommending the removal of David Logan, a justice of the peace from Fayette County, for packing a jury and other alleged malfeasances. The magistrates voted fifteen to five in favor of this action, forming a significant element of the majority.[13]

This vote of the justices of the peace was more than offset by their actions in other cases of alleged misconduct. On seven occasions a majority of voting county court justices

13 *Constitution of 1792*, Art. 3 and Art. 5, sec. 2; *Constitution of 1799*, Art. 4, sec. 6, and Art. 5; *H.J., 1792*, 2d sess., pp. 61–62; *H.J., 1809–1810*, pp. 161–62.

supported efforts to secure conviction of magistrates accused of malfeasance. For example in 1793 they voted five to three to remove William Lamb, a magistrate from Mason County, and in 1795 they were instrumental in overturning a committee recommendation to reject a petition seeking the removal of John McHatton, a magistrate from Scott County. On four other occasions a majority of justices voted with a majority of other legislators to recommend the unseating of a delinquent county magistrate. In another instance seven of ten voting justices supported a motion designed to expedite the removal of a magistrate.[14]

The Senate did not vote on as many resolutions to remove county magistrates as did the House because seldom did citizens petition it to initiate such action; sometimes the representatives to whom the petitions were first directed refused to endorse them and other times accused magistrates resigned rather than prolong the humiliation of a public hearing. In three sample votes on such matters recorded in Senate journals before 1850, the participating magistrates were inconsistent: in 1818 most of them voted, and all who did supported the resolution of removal; in 1836 most of them did not vote, but the two who did favored removal; and in 1846 one supported removal, one opposed it, and the other did not vote.[15] In these three instances all but one of the justices voted against their fellow magistrates, hardly the reaction of a self-interested bloc.

Thus the record of the legislative justices of the peace in cases of allegedly wayward magistrates is not that of a special interest group acting to protect one of its own. Instead, their record manifests a spirit of independent thinking free of undue loyalty to professional cohorts or concern for the

---

[14] *H.J., 1793*, p. 60; *H.J., 1795*, pp. 3, 5, 7; *H.J., 1808–1809*, pp. 253–54; *H.J., 1817–1818*, p. 200; *H.J., 1835–1836*, pp. 358–60; *H.J., 1845–1846*, pp. 265–67; *H.J., 1801*, pp. 109–10.

[15] *S.J., 1817–1818*, p. 170; *S.J., 1835–1836*, p. 443; *S.J., 1845–1846*, pp. 298–301.

establishment of institutional immunity. Similar patterns emerge from an analysis of the magistrates' reactions to efforts to regulate the conduct of the county courts and their personnel. In 1813 the justices in the House voted thirteen to seven against a bill to control more effectively the conduct of county magistrates, while at the same session they supported reform by voting thirteen to seven in favor of legislation expediting the legislative trials of allegedly corrupt court justices. Although a majority of House justices voted against bills introduced in 1828 to prevent justices of the peace from becoming securities in certain cases before local tribunals and to define more precisely the duties of the county courts, many of them supported the reform efforts. Again in 1847 they were evenly divided on a motion to table legislation aimed at curtailing fraud and embezzlement on the part of some of their fellow court members; later in the session they voted nine to seven to defeat such a measure. Only with regard to an effort to limit the number of justices in each county did the magistrates turn in an overwhelmingly negative vote, fourteen to three, a decision supported by most other legislators. Senate magistrates exhibited substantial disunity in five attempts to regulate justices of the peace, county courts, or sheriffs, while generally opposing such measures on four other occasions.[16]

Justices of the peace in the assembly voted on one other category of legislation which indirectly affected their position as governors of the counties: bills "to take the sense of the people as to the propriety of calling a constitutional convention." The Constitution of 1799 provided that a convention could be called only if the legislature passed a law calling for a referendum and the people approved a call in

16 H.J., 1813–1814, pp. 77–78, 193; H.J., 1827–1828, pp. 207–8, 297; H.J., 1846–1847, pp. 283, 505; S.J., 1828–1829, pp. 291–92; S.J., 1829–1830, pp. 162–63; S.J., 1830–1831, pp. 102, 130–32; S.J., 1831–1832, pp. 237–39; S.J., 1832–1833, pp. 174–78; S.J., 1834–1835, pp. 325–27; S.J., 1839–1840, pp. 272–73; S.J., 1844–1845, p. 125.

two successive elections. Since during the last two decades of the system reform of the county courts was generally recognized as a probable objective of a constitutional convention, the justices of the peace of the legislature, had they acted through self-interest, might have been expected to vote against bills authorizing referendums. However, they did not respond in a uniformly negative fashion but manifested the same independence and disunity that they often evidenced with regard to legislation directly related to county government. In seven recorded votes on such bills between 1828 and 1847, House magistrates voted six times narrowly and a seventh time decisively in favor of authorizing a convention vote. As with legislation on county government, the senatorial justices of the peace treated convention bills with more unanimity, decisively opposing bills on three occasions, narrowly supporting bills twice, overwhelmingly approving a bill in another vote, and dividing on the question on still another.[17]

Probably because there were fewer magistrates in the legislature and almost no bloc-voting, criticism of justices serving in the General Assembly abated after 1825 until shortly before the Constitutional Convention of 1849. In 1846 the bipartisan committee of seventy-six legislators specifically complained that justices of the peace were allowed to serve in the legislature. In early 1847 "Bourbon" submitted that the presence of magistrates in the legislature violated the separation of powers doctrine, a chant taken up by the Frankfort *Convention*, a reform-minded newspaper, in March of the same year.[18]

If the magistrates were not generally influenced by con-

17 *H.J., 1828–1829*, p. 81; *H.J., 1833–1834*, pp. 90–91; *H.J., 1834–1835*, p. 138; *H.J., 1835–1836*, p. 86; *H.J., 1837–1838*, pp. 122–23; *H.J., 1845–1846*, p. 100; *H.J., 1846–1847*, pp. 72–73; *S.J., 1828–1829*, p. 76; *S.J., 1833–1834*, p. 72; *S.J., 1834–1835*, p. 97; *S.J., 1835–1836*, p. 135; *S.J., 1836–1837*, p. 130; *S.J., 1845–1846*, p. 92; *S.J., 1846–1847*, p. 53.

18 *Yeoman*, 8 October 1846; 21 January 1847; *Convention*, 27 March 1847.

siderations of professional loyalty (except when voting on their fees), they were equally unmoved by party allegiance. Some semblance of party regularity can be seen in only one of twelve relevant House votes and two of thirteen Senate votes. Moreover, in two of the three indications of party allegiance the loyalty involved only one party, with members of the other party dividing their votes. Finally, on one of the two occasions on which the legislators voted exclusively along party lines, only three magistrates participated in the balloting.[19]

Even though the General Assembly was not ruled by a solid voting bloc of magistrates, it was unwilling to reform the county court system or its officers. It repeatedly rejected bills which would have made the county courts less cumbersome and defeated similar proposals which would have regulated more effectively the activities of sheriffs and constables. If this failure to reform was not the result of a conspiracy of legislative justices of the peace, neither did it stem from concerted efforts of the allegedly more conservative Whig Party, which dominated the General Assembly for all but one session between 1827 and 1851. Fifteen sample votes indicate that with the exception of bills involving constables, Whig legislators favored stricter regulation of county government than did their Democratic adversaries. The Jacksonians appear to have been more willing to reform the local constitution early in the history of the state's two-party system when their popular strength was greatest. As their numbers in the legislature decreased, so did their enthusiasm for regulation. This trend may reflect the fact that many Jacksonian politicians were able to dominate county courts in the 1830s and 1840s while losing out at the polls.[20]

19 *H.J., 1844–1845*, p. 225; *S.J., 1829–1830*, pp. 160–61, 163.
20 The fifteen sample votes concerned four bills to make the county courts less unwieldy and more dependable (*H.J., 1827–1828*, pp. 207–9; *S.J.,*

In sum, two grievances emanated from the relationship of the legislature to the county courts. The first, objection to the presence of magistrates in the General Assembly, diminished as the numbers of legislative justices of the peace declined. The second, the failure of the legislature to remedy any of the deficiencies of the county court system, was more serious and helped produce an atmosphere which prompted constitutional revision in 1849.

1834–1835, pp. 325–27; *S.J., 1839–1840*, pp. 272–73; *S.J., 1844–1845*, p. 125); three bills to regulate justices of the peace (*H.J., 1827–1828*, p. 297; *S.J., 1828–1829*, pp. 291–92; *H.J., 1846–1847*, p. 505); two resolutions to remove justices of the peace from office (*S.J., 1835–1836*, p. 443; *S.J., 1845–1846*, p. 301); a bill to regulate sheriffs (*S.J., 1830–1831*, p. 132); a bill to outlaw the selling of the sheriffalty (*S.J., 1832–1833*, pp. 174–78); a bill to compensate a buyer of a sheriffalty for his losses while in office (*S.J., 1827–1828*, pp. 136–38); two bills to regulate constables (*S.J., 1829–1830*, pp. 162–63; *S.J., 1831–1832*, pp. 238–39); and a bill to prevent fraud and collusion between sheriffs, constables, and defendants (*S.J., 1830–1831*, pp. 130–32). Most of the measures were defeated; only the bills to compensate the buyer of a sheriffalty and one of the resolutions to remove a justice of the peace from office passed.

Chapter 7

TOWN AND COUNTRY

THE COUNTY COURTS had a substantial and sometimes abrasive connection with the towns and cities of antebellum Kentucky. Specific statutes enacted by the legislature between 1796 and 1828 and more general grants of authority enabled the courts and their members to mingle significantly and often provocatively in the affairs of towns. After 1827 some of the larger towns began to gain constitutional immunity from county court interference, yet on several occasions this state of semiautonomy served to heighten rather than reduce tensions between the two local governmental bodies.

A statute of 1796 authorized county courts to establish towns upon petition, to set their boundaries, and to fill vacancies on their boards of trustees should the towns themselves neglect to hold elections. A statute of 1800 appreciably increased the powers of the county courts over towns. The courts were authorized to fix the number of trustees in all towns save fifteen of the largest, to select annually a new board of trustees should any town neglect to hold elections, and to settle annually with the town tax collectors, placing all surplus monies in a special trust fund. Although courts evidently audited the tax accounts of towns within their jurisdiction only rarely, they did periodically appoint town trustees. Finally, a statute of 1828 empowered the county courts to force town trustees to account for all receipts and expenditures in the event they failed to do this on their own.[1]

By virtue of more general grants of authority the county courts opened all new streets within towns and owned and operated the public square, which was the geographical and political center of towns. This ownership produced relationships of both cooperation and controversy between courts and towns. Finally, members of county courts, acting in their capacities as justices of the peace, constituted the principal judicial agents of towns, and other county officials such as the sheriff, the constables, the jailer, and the coroner performed services for them.

An excellent way to determine the realities of the political and constitutional links between county courts and towns is to examine the relationship between Fayette County and its seat, Lexington, commencing in 1782 and culminating with the fight to repeal the city charter in 1836. Such an examination is appropriate because throughout the antebellum period Lexington was one of the principal cities of Kentucky, and Fayette was one of its foremost counties. Although its early predominance in the economy of Kentucky receded in the 1820s, Lexington continued to be the intellectual, political, and social center of the state. Fayette County possessed a government notable for its far-reaching powers and political influence.

The relationship between Fayette County and Lexington between 1782 and 1831 was clearly characteristic of the dominant position of counties in local constitutions. As in most counties, the Fayette court opened all new streets in the county seat, Lexington, and owned and operated the public square upon which the courthouse and other public buildings were located. The court allowed the town to con-

---

[1] *Acts, 1796–1797,* pp. 39–41; *Acts, 1800,* chap. 4, secs. 1, 3, 4; *Acts, 1827–1828,* chap. 71, sec. 1.

struct a market house and an engine house on the public square and to utilize the courthouse for its trustee meetings and the county jail and workhouse for its criminals. In addition, certain members of the court, all of whom acted individually as justices of the peace, constituted the principal judicial officers of the town. These county-town magistrates also occasionally assumed other responsibilities for the town, such as supervising elections. Furthermore, other officials of the county government, such as the sheriff, the constables, the jailer, and the coroner, performed services for Lexington.[2]

The intimate relationship between Lexington and Fayette County produced dissension as well as cooperation. In 1817 the county court ordered the trustees of Lexington to tear down the dilapidated town market house. When the trustees resisted, the members of the court set a deadline for the observance of their order and threatened to instruct the sheriff to do the necessary razing, authorizing him to "summon the strength of the county if required." After this show of determination the trustees acquiesced. Tensions were renewed when at their November court the justices of the peace ordered the town to raze "the old engine house" and made known their intention to petition the legislature for permission to lease that part of the public square upon which the market house had stood. The trustees responded vigorously, voting to send a committee before the court to express their "disapprobation." This maneuver apparently succeeded, for there is no evidence that the town removed the engine house or that the county court petitioned the legislature for permission to lease part of the

2 Littell, *Statute Law*, 3:170–71; Record Book of the Town of Lexington, 1780–1811 (Lexington Municipal Building), pp. 29, 209, 213–15, 235; Lexington Record Book, 1811–1817, pp. 149, 188, 216, 236, 241–42, 259, 267, 278, 288, 336, 363, 373, 385; Lexington Record Book, 1830–1836, p. 91; *Acts, 1795*, chap. 33, sec. 2; *Acts, 1828–1829*, chap. 114, sec. 2.

public square. However, the question of what to do with the vacant ground in the square was still a debated issue during the next decade. In 1822 the town trustees unsuccessfully attempted to persuade the county court and the legislature to permit the ground to be used for a town hall, and in 1826 the justices of the peace again contemplated seeking legislative permission to dispose of the unoccupied area.[3]

Townsmen grumbled over other matters also. They complained that they were forced to pay the county levy as well as city taxes and received few benefits from the county in return. They were especially annoyed when the county court refused in 1817 to contribute to the construction of a mental hospital to be located within the town limits.[4] At times they charged the county magistrates and constables with shirking their duties as the principal judicial and police officers of the community, and on other occasions they accused them of being overly zealous.

The relative weakness of the town in Kentucky during its early history was due not only to the superior constitutional power of the county court but also to the lack of authority vested in town government. This was especially true for Lexington, which was until about 1825 the largest community in the state. Only gradually during the first fifty years of its existence as an established town, from 1782 to 1831, did Lexington attain those powers basic to a viable town government. And for these grants of authority Lexington, like other towns, was dependent upon piecemeal consideration by the legislature. Thus in 1792 the General Assembly, largely incorporating a law enacted by the Virginia legislature two years earlier, granted to the town of

3 Fayette County Court Order Book, 1811–1817, pp. 520, 535 (U.K. microfilm, reel M366:2); Lexington Record Book, 1811–1817, pp. 359, 366–69, 375; Fayette County Court Order Book, 1817–1821, pp. 63, 68 (U.K. microfilm, reel M366:2); Lexington Record Book, 1811–1817, p. 382; Lexington Record Book, 1818–1830, pp. 199, 309.

4 *Gazette*, 14 April, 26 May 1817.

Lexington the right to govern its streets, establish and control a town market house, abate nuisances, and levy taxes not to exceed £100. During the next decade the legislature authorized the town trustees to prohibit horse racing in the streets, impound loose swine within the town limits, hire day and night watchmen, increase the tax base by £50, pave certain streets, and exempt all able-bodied residents from working on county roads.[5]

From 1802 to 1830 the legislature further broadened the still rudimentary powers of the trustees by granting them greater police powers, providing more effective means to prevent fires, expanding their taxing powers, authorizing them to license theaters and tippling houses, and permitting them to borrow up to $20,000 upon the town's credit.[6] However, by 1830 the government of Lexington still lacked a judiciary and a chief executive, as well as other attributes of a semi-independent urban government, such as the right to open new streets and to license taverns, groceries, and other such establishments.

In light of the constitutional deficiencies of town government in Lexington, as well as the inadequacies of those services which the county officials furnished, it is not surprising that efforts were made by the trustees and townsmen to secure greater autonomy. In 1812 the trustees sought partial relief by petitioning the General Assembly for the creation of an independent judiciary. The effort failed. In 1792 they unsuccessfully petitioned the assembly for a charter establishing Lexington as a municipal corporation, and in 1815 they again contemplated such a move but took only preliminary action. Although the legislature could grant charters to towns making them cities and bestowing upon

5 *Acts, 1792,* 1st sess., chap. 10; *Acts, 1793,* chap. 27, sec. 2; *Acts, 1795,* chap. 33, sec. 1; *Acts, 1796–1797,* pp. 111–14; Littell, *Statute Law,* 2:171, 3:35–36.

6 Littell, *Statute Law,* 3:411–12; *Acts, 1810–1811,* chap. 257, sec. 5; Littell, *Statute Law,* 5:512; *Acts, 1822,* chap. 437; *Acts, 1829–1830,* chap. 284.

them more general and complete powers of government, no such grant was made until 1828, when the assembly incorporated Louisville, by then the largest city of the Commonwealth. The success of Louisville's leaders prompted Lexingtonians to petition again for a charter in 1831, and this time they were successful.[7]

Two of the most important provisions of "An Act to Incorporate the City of Lexington," passed by the General Assembly on December 7, 1831, were in section seven, establishing an independent judiciary, and section seventeen, granting city residents immunity from county taxes. The former provision freed the city fathers from dependence upon the county for law enforcement, while the latter not only expanded significantly the city's taxing potential but also eliminated a major grievance which had persisted throughout the period of Lexington's status as a town, namely that town residents paid taxes to the county without receiving significant benefits. Other provisions of the charter practically eliminated the role of the county court in the administration of what had been town business. For example, the city was now authorized to appoint its own food inspectors and to license its taverns, whereas before the county court had taken care of these responsibilities for the entire county. Furthermore, to open new streets the city would now apply to the circuit court, not the county court. Finally, the city fathers were given the authority to eliminate another form of dependence upon the county by a provision empowering them to erect "buildings for a poorhouse and a work-house."[8]

The emancipation of Lexington from the constitutional grip of Fayette County and the commensurate invigoration of city government did not eliminate friction between city

[7] Lexington Record Book, 1811–1817, pp. 16, 271; *H.J., 1792*, pp. 78, 93; *Acts, 1827–1828*, chap. 172; *Acts, 1831–1832*, chap. 633.

[8] *Acts, 1831–1832*, chap. 633, secs. 7, 10, 13, 17.

and county but merely changed the sources of dissension and complaints. Before incorporation Lexington had done most of the remonstrating and Fayette County allegedly had committed most of the grievances; thereafter the roles were reversed. For example, in 1833 the county court unsuccessfully sought to curtail some of Lexington's financial independence by petitioning the legislature for a law which would have applied all fines received by the city court "to the use of the county of Fayette in lessening the county levy." In November 1835 residents of the county, already discontented about certain rulings by the city council, staged an open revolt over a wood ordinance which sought to insure uniformity and honesty in the weighing and selling of wood. Branding themselves as "slaves to the rulers of Lexington" and the wood ordinance as unconstitutional, county residents held a meeting on December 14 and resolved to cease selling wood to Lexington until the "obnoxious ordinance . . . be repealed." [9]

Yet these outbursts of friction between county and city were only preludes to a basic confrontation which occurred in 1836 when dissidents from the county combined with those from the city and attempted to repeal the charter of Lexington. The occasion for the challenge was a decision by Thomas Hickey, judge of the Fayette Circuit Court, holding that the judicial system of Lexington was unconstitutional. In 1831 the General Assembly had granted an independent judiciary to Lexington in a rather peculiar manner. Instead of creating a separate court to be run by a judge, the legislature had vested the city's judicial authority in the mayor, who was also the chief executive of the community. He was given exclusive original jurisdiction in all cases involving violations of city ordinances and concurrent jurisdiction in those civil and criminal cases

[9] *H.J., 1832–1833*, pp. 197–98, 208; *Observer and Reporter*, 30 December 1835.

heard by justices of the peace. His decisions were apparently to be final in cases involving city ordinances but could be appealed to the circuit court in cases involving other civil and criminal matters. The legislature had created a constitutional problem by vesting judicial authority in the mayor. Section twenty-four of the city charter provided that ballots should be cast for at least two candidates for mayor and that the governor should commission, with the advice and consent of the Senate, one of the two candidates receiving the highest number of votes. Since the Constitution provided that all judges were to be commissioned by the governor with the consent of the Senate and were to hold office for life and since the city charter provided that the mayor was to be chosen annually and in large part by the voters of Lexington, it was questionable whether the city court had been constitutionally established.[10]

Oddly enough, no one challenged the validity of section twenty-four until Nelson Turner did so in December 1835, although its shortcomings, as a Lexington newspaper admitted soon thereafter, were glaring. James E. Davis, the mayor, had tried Turner, a farmer and resident of the county, for breach of the peace and had fined him fifty dollars. Turner failed to pay the fine and was imprisoned. In an action brought before Judge Hickey he subsequently denied the validity of his conviction and imprisonment, contending that section twenty-four of the city charter was unconstitutional. In a carefully reasoned and lengthy opinion issued in the latter part of December 1835, Judge Hickey agreed with Turner's contentions, freed him, and rendered invalid and inoperative the City Court of Lexington.[11]

It soon became apparent that this successful challenge to

10 *Acts, 1831*, chap. 633, sec. 7; *Constitution of 1799*, Art. 4, sec. 3.
11 *Intelligencer*, 4 March 1836; *Observer and Reporter*, 23 December 1835; *Gazette*, 9 January 1836.

the validity of a cornerstone of the Lexington city charter was premeditated. A local newspaper reported that Turner had gone to jail in order "to test the constitutionality of the charter." [12] The motives behind this belated test case probably lay in city and county partisan politics as well as in broader constitutional and political rivalries between the two agencies of local government, for it came at a time when the first state two-party system was firmly established and had already produced antagonisms within and between the county and the city. In order to understand the possible motivations underlying *In re Turner* and at the same time to comprehend the more serious questions raised by the case, the realities of party politics in Fayette County and Lexington must be explored.

Judge Hickey was a Democrat and as such was a member of the political party which had dominated the Fayette County Court almost from the inception of a two-party system in Kentucky. The Democratic justices of the peace, whose majority on the court was at first very small, had solidified their hold on county government between 1827 and 1835 by recommending only Jacksonians to fill vacancies. Fayette Democrats were less successful in their efforts to control the government of Lexington, their strength at the polls declining between 1827 and 1835. The annual elections, first for trustees of the town and after 1831 for mayor and councilmen of the city, inevitably resulted in the victory of almost totally anti-Jacksonian slates. This did not mean, however, that campaigns were not spirited. After the town election of January 1829 Democratic politicians accused their political opponents of using fraudulent tactics to win an overwhelming majority of the town's trustees.[13]

In terms of the proportion of votes, if not of winners, the Democrats staged something of a comeback in the town

12 *Observer and Reporter*, 23 December 1835.
13 *Gazette*, 9, 16 January 1829.

elections of 1830. But after 1831 the Democratic vote proportionately declined, and in 1834 the Whigs, like the Democrats at the county level, moved to tighten their control over the city council by eliminating ward voting, thereby capitalizing on their overall strength in the city and minimizing the Democratic domination of the first ward. By the end of 1835 the Jacksonian Democrats controlled the government of Fayette County and the Whigs dominated the government of Lexington, and each party vowed that the other would not preserve its constitutional power without challenge. The Whigs promised "retribution" in the face of proscription by the Democratic county court, and the Jacksonians pledged not to "stand idly by and see the rights of the citizens trampled upon" by the Whigs. Thus partisan politics may have prompted Turner's preconceived testing of the constitutionality of Lexington's judicial arm in the courtroom of Democratic Judge Hickey.[14]

After Judge Hickey's decision striking down the Lexington City Court, the Whigs, or at least those who dominated city government, immediately petitioned the legislature for an amendment to the charter reestablishing a city court on constitutional grounds. In short order the General Assembly enacted a law divorcing the mayor's office completely from the council or any other administrative-legislative agency and making it exclusively the repository of the judicial power of the city. In effect the mayor was now the equivalent of a city judge, to be appointed for life by the governor with the advice and consent of the Senate. Soon after the amendment passed, Governor James T. Morehead, a Whig, not surprisingly commissioned the recently reelected mayor of Lexington, James E. Davis, also a Whig, as the first judicial mayor of the city. The amendment also provided that the city council would elect one of its number

[14] *Acts, 1833–1834,* chap. 508, sec. 3; *Reporter,* 27 July 1831; *Gazette,* 9 January 1829.

president, who would in effect assume the executive responsibilities of the old mayor's office. The heavily Whig
council elected as its president Thomas Hart, a nephew
of Henry Clay's wife and an active member of the Whig
party.[15]

The decision of the circuit court, the amendment to the
city charter that it produced, and the unique features of
that revision obviously provided the Democrats of Fayette
County with considerable political ammunition to fire at
their opponents entrenched in the halls of government in
Lexington. Shortly after the amendment was announced,
the Democrats, led by General John McCalla, a leader of
both the county and the state party and a federal marshal
since Andrew Jackson's accession to the White House, began circulating a petition to the legislature calling for the
complete repeal of the Lexington city charter. At the same
time the Democratic newspaper of the county, the ven-
erable *Kentucky Gazette*, published and edited by another
leading Jacksonian, Daniel Bradford, began castigating the
city government. Bradford had a special ax to grind, as his
enemies would later make clear. A member of the county
court, he had unsuccessfully opposed James Davis for
mayor in the January elections. As one of the magistrates
residing in Lexington, he would stand to gain judicial business if the legislature abolished the chartered government
and with it the city court. On February 6 Bradford's paper
carried news of the petition, a letter from certain "Tax
Payers" accusing the city fathers of pocketing public funds,
and an editorial denouncing the manner in which the
amendment to the charter had been secured. The fight to
repeal Lexington's charter had begun.[16]

At first the proposal to amend the charter had aroused

15 *Observer and Reporter*, 13 January 1836; *Acts, 1835–1836*, chap. 44;
S.J., 1835–1836, p. 201; *Gazette*, 6 February 1836.
16 *Gazette*, 6 February 1836.

little, if any, controversy in the state legislature. But the attempts of the Democrats to annul it quickly produced fireworks. In the end Democratic efforts to enact the Fayette petition into law were easily thwarted since the Whigs, as always, outnumbered their opponents in both houses. What finally emerged from the legislature was something of a compromise: it provided by statute for a special election to be held in Lexington on May 6 and 7 at which time the voters of the city would determine the fate of the charter.[17]

It was apparent that one of the primary confrontations in the prereferendum campaign was between the Democratic county court and the Whig city government as well as between the Democratic and Whig parties. Indeed the power structure of the Democratic party in Fayette County and that of the county court were virtually synonymous; a Whig newspaper commenting on this fact some years later branded the county court a Democratic nominating convention. Bradford provided the propaganda for the battle, and the evidence suggests that some of his colleagues on the county court probably contributed their services, too. Likewise, the Whig leadership of Lexington and Fayette County was in many ways identical to the hierarchy of city government, and this junto was reported to be campaigning actively to retain the city's corporate status.[18]

The theme of city versus county government was thrust into the open when shortly after the charter was amended, several Democratic magistrates tried in vain to oust from the county court James Davis, who was by the end of January both a justice of the peace and judge of the reestablished city court. Davis had been appointed to the county court before the emergence of the two-party system in the state and was one of the few anti-Jacksonian magistrates re-

17 Ibid., 20 February 1836; *Acts, 1835–1836*, chap. 448.

18 *Observer and Reporter*, 26 July 1845; *Gazette*, 13 February, 16 June, 25 July 1836.

maining. Supporters of the move to replace him argued that he could not constitutionally serve two masters. The expediency of their argument is apparent when one realizes that Davis, first elected mayor in January 1835, had been serving two masters for over a year without complaint.[19]

Furthermore, much of the debate carried on in public meetings and in the newspapers emphasized that the central issue of the conflict was county versus city government. Advocates of the charter continually referred to this theme by predicting dire consequences for Lexingtonians if the balance of power once again shifted in favor of the county court. At a public meeting held shortly before the special election, a prominent Whig lawyer, Daniel Mayes, defended the charter by noting that a return to town status and the abolition of the mayor's court would place "the administration of the laws, and the peace and good order" of the city into the hands of the county court, whose responsibilities were at best "divided and diluted." To those who complained that under the amended charter the people had no voice in the selection of the city judge, Mayes retorted that at least the judge was selected by the governor with the consent of the Senate, whereas the county court was almost exclusively self-perpetuating. He also warned that the county court would once again begin taxing Lexingtonians should they voluntarily give up their corporate status.[20]

Detractors of the charter denounced the alleged severity of punishments meted out by the mayor while acting in his judicial capacity. They argued that the slightest breach of the peace often resulted in confinement in the city workhouse and heavy fines, implying that the county magistrates were more just. It was suggested that the court costs of the

[19] Fayette County Court Order Book, 1833–1836 (U.K. microfilm, reel M366:5), p. 431; *Gazette*, 13 February 1836.

[20] *Intelligencer*, 3 May 1836.

mayor's tribunal were much higher than those extracted by justices of the peace, and familiar charges were heard denouncing the mayor and his police for their inability to curtail an increasing number of crimes committed within the city. Supporters of the city charter countered these arguments by suggesting that their opponents were inconsistent in complaining on the one hand about stiff penalties and on the other about a soaring crime rate. In fact, they argued, county law officers had been lax in enforcing town ordinances, and since incorporation and the establishment of an independent urban judicial force, the incidence of crime had receded.[21]

The partisan nature of the struggle was apparent, too. Of eleven identifiable leaders of the fight to preserve the charter, nine were Whigs. Of six avowed leaders of the movement to repeal the charter, all but one were Democrats. The two Democrats who helped lead the procharter movement had vested interests in their cause, being the only two Democratic members of the city council. Conversely, the only Whig who belonged to the leadership opposing the charter had been defeated in January for a position on the city council and soon thereafter had failed to secure reappointment as the city tax assessor, a post he had held for seven years.

It was also evident that party considerations had caused certain anticharter leaders to take stands which were inconsistent with former positions. Daniel Bradford, for one, had earlier opposed an abortive effort to repeal the city charter stemming from dissatisfaction with the administration of Mayor Davis. Bradford had condemned that move by dissident Democrats as an extreme way to oust an unwanted mayor. Why not wait, he had asked rhetorically, until the coming elections? This was the same argument used by

21 *Gazette*, 27 February, 5, 26 March 1836; *Observer and Reporter*, 16 March, 4 May 1836; *Intelligencer*, 3, 6 May 1836.

proponents of the charter during the prereferendum campaign. Nor had Bradford ever voiced opposition to the charter during his unsuccessful campaign for the mayoralty the preceding year. Furthermore, he had served as city clerk in 1835, drawing a salary of $250 and, according to his critics, relying almost completely on his deputy to perform the duties of his office.[22] Another leading repealer, Dr. Caleb W. Cloud, had served for many years on the board of trustees and later the city council of Lexington. He had introduced a motion in 1822 protesting the attempt of the county court to dispose of part of the public square.[23] Ironically, he had sponsored the resolution calling for amendments to the charter following Judge Hickey's decision invalidating the city judiciary. But he had failed to win reelection to the council in January 1836 and his defeat, doubtless coupled with his active membership in the Democratic party, placed him in the front ranks of those seeking to abolish the city charter.

Although both sides claimed to have support from the residents of the county, who would not vote in the election but whose sympathy was undoubtedly of psychological value, it is clear that many of Fayette County's farmers sided with the repealers. Doubtless the recent city ordinances which sought to regulate the selling of butter and wood and the other activities affecting the agrarian entrepreneur, who was dependent upon Lexington for his market, had created a hostility which was easily preyed upon by the leaders of repeal. Throughout the campaign preceding the referendum, residents of the county aired their frustrations in letters to the *Gazette*. One "Citizen of Fayette County" wrote that the interests of county and city were "inseparably united" and that the "country people" were deeply

[22] *Gazette*, 22 August 1835; *Observer and Reporter*, 16 March, 4 May 1836; *Intelligencer*, 4 May 1836.
[23] Lexington Record Book, 1818–1830, p. 199.

offended by the extravagances of the amended city charter. Another correspondent denounced the amended charter as well as the recent city ordinances and predicted that Lexington's "aristocrats" would soon pass "an ordinance requiring the farmer to take off his hat, and make his bow to the honorable Mayor and Councilmen when he chanced to meet them." A third commentator from the country argued that "the cause of the confusion and loss of good feeling and harmony among the inhabitants of the city and country, have arisen from the power either given to your Charter of Incorporation" or to those who had obtained "high places of authority" under it.[24]

On May 6 the debating stopped and the voting commenced, carrying over into the next day. In its issue of May 9 Bradford's *Gazette* announced that the "agony is over" and conceded defeat. Lexingtonians had voted to retain the charter, 379 to 323. Although Bradford expressed some bitterness and predicted that the citizens of his city would be "harassed by weekly Mayor's courts," he nonetheless pledged to "cease active operations against the Charter."[25]

Despite Bradford's declaration, he and his fellow Democrats did not end their efforts to change the constitution of the city. They simply tempered their demands by stressing the need for revisions rather than outright repeal. On June 16 William Stanhope, a leading county Democrat and a member of the county court, announced his candidacy for the legislature, expressing his intention, if elected, to seek amendments to Lexington's charter. He particularly cited the need to reform the urban judiciary by curtailing court costs and unnecessary personnel and to restore ward representation on the city council, a system which would allow the Democratic first ward more leverage on election day. On July 25 Bradford published a letter from William Boon,

24 *Gazette,* 5, 12, 19 March 1836.
25 Ibid., 9 May 1836.

senior member of the county court and a leading Democrat, despairing that the breach between the county and city had not been healed. Boon complained of the high cost of doing judicial business in the city court and went so far as to contrast the humane treatment of stray animals by county officials with the allegedly harsh practices perpetrated by city employees.[26]

On August 1 Bradford and others endorsed Stanhope and other candidates for the legislature who proposed amendments to the charter. In the same issue the editor accused the Whigs of refusing to meet with General Mc-Calla and the leaders of reform to discuss charter revisions, which he contended had been promised by charterites during the prereferendum campaign to secure wavering votes. Bradford persisted in making this claim even after the legislative candidates whom he supported had been defeated. Finally, on August 15, the *Gazette* published a letter from "Amicus" announcing the formation of a committee of charterites whose purpose it would be to discuss needed revisions to the city constitution. Shortly thereafter the two sides met and agreed upon certain reforms to be submitted to the legislature as amendments to the charter. Without apparent controversy the General Assembly enacted the proposals into law early in its next session. The act of December 14, 1836, created a separate judge of the city court, returned the responsibilities of chief executive to the mayor rather than to a president of the council, an office which was abolished, eliminated the jurisdiction of the city court over civil matters, and restored the ward system of representation to the city council.[27]

The reforms of December 1836 certainly obviated many of the grievances harbored by opponents of the Lexington charter. The ease with which they were agreed upon by

26 Ibid., 16 June, 15 July 1836.
27 Ibid., 1, 8, 15 August 1836; *Acts, 1836–1837*, chap. 1.

political leaders of the city and county and then converted into law by the legislature suggests that had both sides been more conciliatory and less ambitious at an earlier time, the fight to repeal the charter could have been avoided. On the other hand, there were basic conflicts in the beginning. The transformation of the mayor of Lexington into a judge for life had presented the leaders of Fayette County government and certain out politicians in the city with a rare opportunity to strike a deadly blow at the growing autonomy of Lexington and simultaneously to regain political and constitutional power. Compromise was really not possible until the prolonged confrontation between competing politicians, parties, and governments had been resolved behind the scenes, in the newspapers, and at the polls.

These frictions between Lexington and Fayette County were not unique in the history of the relations between county and city government during the period of the old county court system. An even mightier struggle involved the state's largest city and county. In early 1835 certain ambitious politicians sought to capitalize on disharmony between city and county officials by attempting to have Louisville secede from Jefferson County and secure legislative authorization to form a separate county. The disagreement between the Jefferson County Court and the city of Louisville stemmed from the dilapidated condition of the buildings in the city shared by the two governmental agencies and owned by the county as custodian of the public square. Both the city and the county recognized the need to erect new structures, but they could not agree on how to fund the project. The magistrates favored construction on the site of the old buildings to be financed jointly and equally by the city and the county. The councilmen rejected this proposal and instead demanded either that the county alone pay for the new buildings or that the magistrates transfer to the city the title to the public square, with the city then paying for the construction. The magistrates denounced both of these plans, arguing that the first was inequitable and that the second was a veiled attempt to usurp control of the public buildings and drive the county court off the public square.[28]

The inability of local officials to settle their differences increased the frustration of the public and prompted efforts in January 1835 to secure a legislative act making Louisville a separate county. It is apparent that supporters of this move had more in mind than constitutional reform. The Louisville *Public Advertiser*, a Democratic newspaper, charged that the separatist movement was inspired by frustrated officeseekers who, having failed to secure positions in Jefferson County, were now seeking to create new offices which they themselves would fill. Furthermore, the *Advertiser* asserted, these conspirators desired to oust from office the Pope family and its allies, whom they falsely accused of controlling the county and circuit courts.[29]

Regardless of whether they dominated the county court, the Popes and their friends did control the leadership of the Jacksonian party of Jefferson County, the clerkships of the circuit and county courts, the deputy clerkship of the county court, the offices of county jailer and commonwealth's attorney, and the postmastership of Louisville. Since most of the Popes resided within the city, they would either have to move or resign their offices if Louisville were made a separate county. The Whig newspaper, the Louisville *Journal*, provided evidence that the *Advertiser's* accusations were correct when it expressed its "regret" that the Pope family was "not prolific enough to furnish a great

---

28 The best summaries of the background to the Louisville–Jefferson County dispute are in the Louisville *Public Advertiser*, 3 January, 6, 14 February 1835; see also Jefferson County Court Order Book, 1831–1834 (U.K. microfilm, in process), pp. 313–14; Jefferson County Court Order Book, 1834–1838 (U.K. microfilm, in process), pp. 28, 38–40, 48–49, 56–58, 74.

29 Ibid., 3, 12 January 1835; *H.J., 1834–1835*, pp. 143, 290.

lazy, lubberly boy for every office, not only in the city and county, but throughout the state," and then less facetiously endorsed city-county separation and the notion that the Popes should move or compete with the rest of the city politicians for places in the new county government.[30]

Throughout the latter part of January and the early part of February debate raged in the two newspapers over the merits and motives of the proposed separation. The Democratic journal accused the city politicians of attempting to steal the public square, the courthouse, and the county records by unconstitutionally destroying Jefferson County. The newspaper further argued that separation would only heighten tensions between city and county and would greatly augment the tax burden of Louisvillians. The Whig paper countered that the proposed separation was valid and that the public square and its buildings would rightfully belong to the newly created county.[31]

In the face of this challenge to their very existence, members of the county court strove for compromise with the city councillors. The two bodies appointed a joint committee to study the problem of new facilities and on February 14 announced an agreement whereby a building to be funded equally by the city and the county would be constructed either on the public square or on another site. The House of Representatives was apparently unimpressed by this development and on February 25 narrowly passed the bill to make Louisville a separate county. However, the Senate averted a potential constitutional and political crisis when it allowed the bill to lapse.[32]

---

[30] *Public Advertiser*, 13 January 1835; Louisville *Journal*, quoted in *Public Advertiser*, 13 January 1835.

[31] *Public Advertiser*, 12, 13, 14, 15 January 1835; Louisville *Journal*, quoted in *Public Advertiser*, 12, 13, 14, 15 January 1835.

[32] *Public Advertiser*, 14 February 1835; *H.J., 1834–1835*, pp. 367–68; *S.J., 1834–1835*, p. 385. The bill reached the Senate on February 25, was read twice and ordered read a third time, but never again was considered.

Between 1833 and early 1849 the legislature incorporated two cities and fifteen towns and gave to each governmental powers which had formerly been exercised by the county courts. The city of Maysville, incorporated in early 1833, was given the same privileges as Louisville and Lexington, including an independent judiciary, immunity from county taxation, and the rights to license various retail establishments and to appoint food inspectors. The city of Covington, incorporated one year later, was granted the same powers and benefits save tax immunity. Thereafter the General Assembly incorporated fifteen towns, giving to each an independent judiciary and to many powers to license retail stores and to construct their own public buildings. Furthermore, during the last decade of the old county court system the legislature granted independent judiciaries to twenty other towns.[33]

Even though each of these legislative bequests represented an encroachment upon the power of county courts, they produced no outbursts like those in Lexington and Louisville. Indeed the other recorded disputes between county courts and towns in antebellum Kentucky were minor in comparison with the attempts to revoke the charter of Lexington and to separate Louisville from Jefferson County. Between 1838 and 1848, for example, the Bracken County Court and the trustees of Augusta waged a legal battle over the ownership of the public square of the former county seat, a confrontation hardly approaching the significance of attempted secession or revocation.[34]

The fight to repeal the charter of Lexington and the battle to make Louisville a separate county are significant in several ways. Both represent basic conflicts between city

33 *Acts, 1832–1833*, chap. 197; *Acts, 1833–1834*, chap. 505.
34 Bracken County Court Order Book, 1835–1845, pp. 128, 143, and Bracken County Court Order Book, 1846–1851, p. 150 (U.K. microfilm, reels M478:121–22); *Trustees of Augusta* v. *Perkins*, 3 B. Monroe 437 (1843) and 8 B. Monroe 207 (1848).

and county government and between ambitious men attached to those governments. The struggle in Lexington demonstrates how competing politicians in control of separate constitutional vehicles used those vehicles to further their own political goals. The crisis in Louisville illustrates how out politicians seized on intergovernmental conflict to further their own designs. Both illuminate the recurring theme in American history of tension between country folk and city folk. And finally, both reveal that struggles over the local constitutions of antebellum Kentucky involved much more than institutional bickering and were inseparable from political intrigue and personal aggrandizement.

Chapter 8

DEFICIENCIES
AND REFORM

THE COUNTY COURT SYSTEM of antebellum Kentucky was replete with institutional deficiencies, which along with the frictions of politics caused its downfall at midcentury. Inattentiveness, cumbersomeness, disorderliness, and inexpertness pervaded the local tribunals.

The ever-increasing numbers of justices of the peace and county courts and the lack of a general requirement that each member of the court be present at terms other than those set aside to certify claims and district roads produced widespread complaints that many of the magistrates frequently failed to attend their monthly courts or were not punctual. One critic argued that it was necessary to "hunt [the justices] down in the courtyard" to get them to hold a court. A correspondent to the Frankfort *Kentucky Yeoman* in 1848 wrote that it was frequently difficult for courts to summon a quorum when it was necessary to have a majority present to transact business. W. C. Marshall, delegate from Bracken County to the Constitutional Convention of 1849, reiterated this complaint, suggesting that the failure of the state to pay the magistrates for their services on the court accounted for their inattention to duties.[1]

Although such complaints were probably exaggerated, there is no question that county courts sometimes could not transact business because of a lack of a quorum. In January

1834, for example, the Fayette County Court was forced to postpone action on an application for a renewal of a tavern license because a majority of its members was not present. The problem was chronic in Barren County. Thomas A. Edmunds attempted for eight consecutive months to renew his tavern license with the county court but failed because at all the terms save one the court lacked a majority of its membership; at the court of claims, when such a quorum was present, the tribunal was so pressed with business that it did not have time to accede to his request. As a result the circuit court fined Edmunds for operating a tavern without a license.[2]

A few courts fined members who were absent without cause; more often, however, the delinquent justices were summoned and promptly excused or fined and subsequently released from the fines. Some courts encouraged inattentive and nonattending magistrates to resign and recommended replacements who, it was hoped, would better serve their neighbors. At least one court which had been sorely hampered by the persistent lack of a quorum went so far as to advertise in the local newspaper calling on its missing members to appear. Most courts, however, seemed content to ignore the problem.[3]

One further judicial check should be noted. The circuit courts were empowered to fine members of the county courts should the latter not perform certain duties, such as fixing tavern rates and districting the public roads. Like the others, this restraint seems not to have been effective since circuit courts seldom fined magistrates, and when they

1 *Yeoman*, 28 September 1848; *Proceedings*, p. 697.

2 Fayette County Court Order Book, 1833–1836, p. 21 (U.K. microfilm, reel M366:5); petition of Thomas A. Edmunds to Governor John Breathitt, 20 March 1833, Breathitt Papers, jacket 335 (G.P., reel 37).

3 Bourbon County Court Order Book, 1808–1812, pp. 464, 468 (U.K. microfilm, reel M277:1738–39).

did, governors, exercising their constitutional power, frequently remitted the fines.

Compounding the problems of attendance were those caused by the enormous expansion of membership on the courts. Even the smallest courts usually had at least ten members, while most had from fifteen to twenty-five. The tendency of the legislature to increase the number of justices of the peace did meet the needs of the people for additional representation and more single magistrates but at the same time rendered the county courts even more cumbersome. This caused many problems, as did the lack of a requirement that members attend court except on a few specified occasions and their tendency to sit for only part of a session. One correspondent to the *Yeoman* pictured a typical county court as a scene of "confusion and disorder," and when Francis M. Bristow, delegate from Todd County to the Constitutional Convention of 1849, announced that "every gentleman knows that the court is unwieldly," no one protested. The "duty of all to attend, but the special duty of none—the business of every one, and no one in particular" meant that individual magistrates often heard only portions of cases before rendering judgments or voting on orders. An even number of justices sitting on a court sometimes produced split decisions and further delayed final action. In order to avoid this confusion most lawyers and clients preferred to appear before a sparsely populated bench than a particularly well-attended session.[4]

Such strategy could aid individual litigants but did very little to ameliorate the problem. Members of the legislature attempted from time to time to deal with these grievances, but to no avail. In 1810 the House of Representatives rejected a bill which would have authorized each county court

---

[4] *Yeoman*, 28 September 1848; *Proceedings*, pp. 697–99, 711; Fayette County Court Order Book, 1833–1836, p. 292 (U.K. microfilm, reel M366:5).

to appoint one of its members president in order to afford
some sort of executive direction to the unwieldy institution. In 1828 the House defeated a much more comprehensive attempt at reform; the rejected measure provided
that each county court should annually divide its members
into three classes, each of which would be alternately responsible for holding court except for those terms during
which the statutes required the presence of a majority of
the magistrates. Stiffer penalties for nonattendance would
also have been provided. In 1835 and 1840 the Senate voted
down bills which would have required each county court
to allocate annually almost all its duties to just three of its
members, reforms which might have obviated a major cause
of unwieldiness. Finally, in 1837, the lower house con-
curred in the report of its committee for courts of justice
that it was "inexpedient" to draft and consider a bill "com-
pelling by law the attendance of each and every member"
of the county courts at "each and every term of said courts." [5]

Another grievance closely related to the awkward nature
of the county court system was the inability of its personnel
to maintain order in the courtroom. A foreign correspondent to the *Kentucky Gazette* styling himself "A Hibernian
Visitor" and touring the state in the spring of 1804 found
that the county courts exhibited "an unfavorable example
of republican order." He characterized their proceedings as
scenes of lawyers "wrangling and disputing among themselves," litigants "often clamorous," witnesses "pertinacious
and contemptuous," and droves of spectators "drawn together [more] from a spirit of curiosity, than on an account
of business . . . of their own . . . , some sober and others
drunk, laughing, talking, sometimes shouting, and not un-
frequently brawling and fighting." The Irish observer

[5] *H.J., 1809–1810*, p. 209; *H.J., 1827–1828*, pp. 207–9; *S.J., 1834–1835*, pp.
325–27; *S.J., 1839–1840*, pp. 272–73; *H.J., 1837–1838*, pp. 68, 127.

blamed this excessive display of the "democratick notions of independence" on the permissiveness of the justices and suggested that in Europe "such disorder and . . . licentiousness" would not be tolerated. John Bradford, editor of the *Gazette,* endorsed these remarks and lamented that Kentucky's courtrooms were "among the worst examples of republican 'order and decorum.' " [6]

A few courts moved to correct this deficiency. At the first meeting of the Boyle County Court in March 1842, the assembled justices issued the following rules of procedure and decorum:

1. The senior justice shall preside in court and in his absence the next eldest and so on in regular order throughout.

2. The presiding justice for the time being shall decide points of order. All motions shall be addressed to him, and all orders, judgments or appointments shall be announced through him.

3. All motions shall come from the bar and shall be made in the following order. The attorney for the county shall be first called upon; the next attorney on the list shall be next called upon and so on to the foot of the list, and lastly citizens or other persons having business in court and choosing to make their own motions.

4. To enable the court to carry into effect the 3rd rule the clerk at the commencement of each term shall furnish the presiding justice for the time being with a list of names of the lawyers admitted to practice at this bar; which list shall be made out in order of admission the first admitted standing first on the list after the county attorney and so on throughout.

6 *Gazette,* 27 March 1804.

5. Any member of the court wishing to address the court shall rise to his feet and address the presiding justice for the time being.

6. In the appointment of officers when there are more than one person in nomination the court shall vote by ballot delivered to the presiding justice who shall count the votes and announce the appointment and when the court are equally divided shall give the casting vote in which case alone he shall be entitled to vote.

7. This Court will appoint no one to office who engages in the practice of electioneering and tampering with the members of the court for such appointment.

8. The clerk shall keep a regular docket of all motions and appeals pending which shall at each term be regularly called and each case tried, dismissed or continued.

9. No member of this court after taking his seat on the bench at any term will be allowed to absent himself without leave.

10. No member of the court while in session will be allowed to converse either publickly or privately with persons other than members of the court and with them only in consultation as to the matter before the court and shall give their attention exclusively to the business before the court.[7]

It is evident that these rules were designed to keep order on the bench as well as in the courtroom, but it is not known whether they were successfully implemented.

Despite the relatively high socioeconomic status of most of the justices of the peace, it is apparent that many of them lacked the kind of dedication necessary for a system of

[7] Boyle County Court Order Book, 1842–1847, pp. 7–8 (U.K. microfilm, reel M311:2031–32).

county government such as theirs to succeed. Indeed the quality of their performance was at issue throughout the antebellum period. Discussion of this situation was especially intense during the years preceding the second and third state constitutional conventions and at the latter conclave. Many of the commentators argued that the county magistrates were at best mediocre and at worst inept. "A Farmer," agitating in the *Gazette* in 1794 for a new state Constitution, contended that the members of the county courts were poorly educated and implicitly inferior in terms of "nature, acquired abilities [and] worth or intelligence." While he admitted that a few were gentlemen whose "philanthropy, politeness and intelligence do honor to human nature," he argued that most were mediocre. The "Hibernian Visitor" corresponding to the same newspaper in 1804 blamed the sorry condition of the state's judiciary in part on the fact that the justices were men "not generally selected from the most respectable and best informed citizens." He found that "many of them are very ignorant, some of them are not respected in their neighborhood, and [there are] others whose moral character will not bear scrutiny or investigation." Nearly half a century later delegates to the Constitutional Convention of 1849 seconded these views. Larkin J. Proctor, delegate from Lewis County, submitted that the county courts were "composed of men, many of whom were incompetent to discharge the duties of their office" and that the probability of obtaining justice before such a tribunal was about as certain as "a game of chance." Ira Root, delegate from Campbell County, condemned "the ignorance of the magistracy," and W. C. Marshall, delegate from Bracken County, compared them to jackasses.[8]

Not all the analysts of the county courts wholly condemned them, however. An anonymous critic who was generally disparaging of the courts in a letter to the *Kentucky*

[8] *Gazette*, 1 March 1794, 27 March 1804; *Proceedings*, pp. 699, 703, 709.

Yeoman in 1848 conceded that "the best men in the community may be, and generally are, [their] members," while G. W. Johnston, delegate from Shelby County to the Constitutional Convention of 1849, asserted that the members of the courts were usually "well qualified." Others saw an unfortunate unevenness in the caliber of the magistrates. One delegate, Francis M. Bristow, observed that while some of the justices of the peace were "wholly unqualified to discharge [their] duties," others were "excellent men"; and Charles Chambers, delegate from Boone County, submitted that the justices of his own county were "all men of good character, fair capacity and sound integrity," implying that this was not always true in other parts of the state.[9]

It is, of course, impossible to judge the relative intelligence of the magistrates. A few petitions and other documents written by magistrates are scattered throughout the governors' papers; some are obviously the products of semi-literate minds, but others were certainly drafted by the well-educated. Beyond these few examples there is only peripheral information. Certainly, if the county court judges were willing and able, they could usually draw upon adequate courthouse libraries to bolster their knowledge of the law. Most of these depositories were as well supplied as any of the judicial tribunals in the state, usually containing full sets of the legislative acts and journals, the printed decisions of the Court of Appeals, digests of state law, and incomplete collections of the acts of Congress.[10] Yet it is apparent from much of the criticism directed at the magistrates that they were too often unwilling to perform their responsibilities, no matter what their capabilities and resources might have been.

[9] *Yeoman*, 28 September 1848; *Proceedings*, pp. 697, 709, 712.

[10] For inventories and other papers relating to county court library holdings see Isaac Shelby Papers, jacket 115 (G.P., reel 16); Thomas Metcalfe Papers, jacket 302 (G.P., reel 34); William Owsley Papers, jacket 570 (G.P., reel 84).

Too few of the magistrates, most of whom were not lawyers, were willing to engage in the requisite study and reflection necessary to familiarize themselves with the many legal specialties within the jurisdiction of the county courts. Their performance as judges was at best uneven. All too often, as the Court of Appeals announced in 1829, the record of the local tribunals upon review revealed numerous blunders. Indeed critics averred that litigants appealed decisions of county courts more often than those of any other tribunal. During the twilight of the second state Constitution, county courts were especially castigated for their allegedly inept implementation of the probate laws. "Philodemos," writing in the *Yeoman* in December 1846, found the existing probate system far too complex and cumbersome. Executors and administrators had to wait weeks, even months, before gaining authority to administer estates, and thereafter devisees and heirs had to wait even longer before receiving their distributions. "Bourbon" reiterated the complaints of "Philodemos" shortly afterward and queried, "How long shall it be before a villainous county court system shall give way to an enlightened probate court!" The editor of the Flemingsburg *Fleming Flag* denounced the county court probate system, saying that its extravagance and abuse exhausted small estates. He pictured the probate agents of county courts, the commissioners, appraisers, criers, clerks, lawyers, administrators, and executors as parasites feeding on the assets of the estate until very little was left.[11]

Not surprisingly, these deficiencies prompted agitation for reform of the county court system. Indeed such efforts were made almost as soon as the system had been codified by the Kentucky legislature. In 1794 "a Farmer" wrote a lengthy letter to the *Gazette* denouncing the county mag-

11 *Commonwealth for Robbins v. Williams*, 1 J. J. Marshall 308 (1829); *Yeoman*, 17 December 1846, 21 January 1847; Flemingsburg *Fleming Flag*, quoted in *Convention*, 9 January, 1 May 1847.

istrates and by implication calling for changes in the Constitution which would prohibit them from serving in the
General Assembly. Not only were the justices of the peace
dominating the legislative branch of the state government,
according to the correspondent, but they were also counsel-
ing the governor and thus were in effect an aristocratic
cabal running both state and local governments. "Why shall
we suffer them to lord it over us with the pre-eminence of
such dangerous, complicated and extensive powers?" he
asked. At the very least, he continued, the voters should reject these "petty tyrants" at the next election. Several
months later another correspondent to the *Gazette* warmly
endorsed "Farmer's" sentiments and more expressly called
for a constitutional convention.[12]

These initial efforts for a repudiation of the justices at
the polls were unsuccessful, nor did this early protest result in the desired reforms at the Constitutional Convention
of 1799. While that conclave did alter the Constitution with
respect to the county courts, the changes strengthened rather
than weakened the political leverage of the magistrates. The
justices were not prohibited from serving in the legislature
and in effect were given the right to fill vacancies on the
county courts, a privilege which had formerly been exclusively possessed by the governor and the Senate. Most of
the deliberation at the convention appears to have been
directed toward protecting slavery, securing the popular
election of state senators, and preserving an independent judiciary, the latter reform bolstering the position of the justices of the peace.

Public protest against the county courts generally abated
during the next four decades. There were isolated outbursts,
such as that from the "Hibernian Visitor" in 1804, but no
constitutional reform was seriously considered until 1837.
In that year the legislature authorized a statewide poll to be

12 *Gazette*, 4 March, 4 October 1794.

held in August 1838 on the question of whether to convene another constitutional convention. Many supporters of a convention in the assembly were seeking basic changes in the system of couty courts. Senator Archibald Dixon of Henderson County asserted that "nearly the whole people of the State are . . . opposed to the present county court system" and advocated an alteration in the Constitution allowing the voters "every six or ten years, to purge the judicial bench" of incompetents. John L. Helm, representative from Hardin County, denounced the self-perpetuating nature of the courts which allowed "unqualified men to remain in office" and proposed that magistrates be elected or at least appointed for a limited term.[13]

Convention opponents rallied to the defense of the courts, asserting that any defects could be remedied by the legislature. Robert Nelson Wickliffe, editor of the Lexington *Observer and Reporter*, argued that the legislature had "heaped upon the county courts" so many responsibilities that they could not perform all of them efficiently and that it was up to the legislature rather than a constitutional convention to remedy faults in the system. Others equated proposals to elect members of the county courts with plans to abolish an independent judiciary, a prospect they viewed with horror. The inefficiency of the early sheriffs of the state was cited as proof that elected county officials functioned even worse than appointed ones.[14]

Many Whigs opposed a convention, fearing that it would undo their carefully gerrymandered legislative and congressional districts and undermine their solid control of state politics. Even certain leading Democrats disapproved of a convention because they feared that it would work the people "up into a feverish state." Some of these men, including Daniel Bradford and Matthews Flournoy, both of

13 Ibid., 8 February 1838; *Commonwealth*, 11 April 1838.
14 *Gazette*, 18 January 1838; *Intelligencer*, 24 July 1838.

Fayette County, doubtless opposed constitutional reform because they themselves were county magistrates. Finally, the fact that abolitionists generally supported a convention poisoned such a call in the eyes of both party organizations. It is therefore not surprising that the voters soundly defeated the attempt to authorize another constitutional convention. Of over 100,000 votes cast in 1838, fewer than 27,000 endorsed the proposal, far below the majority needed.[15]

The defeat of efforts to reform the Constitution in 1838 did not end outcries against the county court system. In his opinion to the secretary of state in October 1840, Attorney General O. G. Cates expressed deep dissatisfaction not only with the practice of awarding the sheriffalty to the senior member of the county court but also with the nature of county government. He argued that the "system of *county court jurisprudence*" did not produce a county officialdom of "wise sober discreet intelligent men" as it was intended to do. Five years later the editor of the Paris *Western Citizen* attacked the courts as antirepublican and called for their abolition.[16]

During the remaining years of the 1840s agitation for county court reform accelerated. Colonel Elisha Smith, representative to the legislature from Rockcastle County, described the organization of the courts as "at war with acknowledged principles of our government." The *Yeoman* depicted "an odious county court system which is at variance with the very first principles of our national and state governments" because legislative, judicial, and executive

[15] Mathias, "The Turbulent Years of Kentucky Politics," p. 328; *Gazette*, 1 February, 22 March 1838; Carl R. Fields, "Making Kentucky's Third Constitution" (Ph.D. diss., Univ. of Ky., 1951), pp. 25–26; *Commonwealth*, 5 December 1838.

[16] O. G. Cates to James Harlan, 17 October 1840, Robert Letcher Letterbook, pp. 2–5 (G.P., reel 54); Paris *Western Citizen*, quoted in *Yeoman*, 11 December 1845.

departments were all "centered in this most obnoxious, self-creative, self-elective, and self-perpetuating" body. Writing to the Frankfort *Commonwealth* in December 1846, a "Democrat" endorsed a constitutional amendment providing for the election of all county officers.[17]

In October 1846 the bipartisan committee of seventy-six legislators which issued a proclamation calling for a constitutional convention expressly approved a general overhaul of the county courts. The manifesto contended that "if experience has not pointed out the necessity of a change in our county court system, then we despair of proving anything by experience." The legislators advocated changing the mode of selecting justices, limiting their term of office, and defining their districts of residence so as to eliminate geographical malapportionment.[18] Early in 1847 the legislature, partly in response to the growing pressure for changes in the county court system, once again authorized a referendum on whether to summon a constitutional convention.

Opposition to the courts mounted throughout 1847 as voters prepared to participate in the first round of two electoral mandates necessary to convene a convention. The courts were openly denounced as centers of nepotism. Candidates for the legislature, sensing a popular issue, began to endorse county governmental reform. Early in the year Robert C. McKee, himself a member of the Franklin County Court, inaugurated a newspaper called the *Convention* to promote the cause of constitutional reform, especially the reform of local government. The newspaper lashed the courts unmercifully, accusing them of fostering the sale of public office, nepotism, malapportionment, incompetency, and the misappropriation of tax funds.[19]

17 *Yeoman*, 8 October 1846; *Commonwealth*, 21 April, 29 December 1846.
18 *Yeoman*, 8 October 1846.
19 Ibid., 21 January 1847; *Convention*, 30 January, 27 March, 10 April, 8 May 1847.

Once again leaders of the established order rose to defend the Constitution. Many were local officeholders and not a few, allegedly, were justices of the peace. At the convention of 1849, Ben Hardin recalled that when he first took the stump in behalf of constitutional reform, "the office-holders . . . followed me round and spoke." When he addressed an audience at Bardstown, he was "haunted by the clerks and their families," but this time their efforts were unsuccessful. The Whig party, which had been a bastion of defense against a call in 1838, was now seriously divided over the issue. The specter of emancipation dissipated in the face of denials by proconvention speakers that they intended to tamper with the peculiar institution. The internal improvements binge of the 1830s and 1840s and the increased taxation that it provoked prompted many to demand constitutional curbs on state spending. Furthermore, more and more politicians claimed that their constituents demanded democratization not only of county government but of the entire judiciary as well.[20]

Equally important, abuses of the county court system seemed to have multiplied. The emergence of party politics in Kentucky had intensified the oligarchical nature of the county courts and thus had made them even less responsive to the people and more vulnerable to the attacks of the reformers. Control of courts by parties unsuccessful at the polls frustrated party politicians. Judicial malapportionment, which expanded markedly after the appearance of two parties, troubled both leaders and constituents. Organized competition for domination of local government lengthened the tenure of justices of the peace and restricted mobility of aspirants for political office. Entrenched factions in county courts seemed to stress loyalty over performance, a state of affairs which may have hastened the decline in the quality of local government. The main goal of magisterial

---

[20] *Convention*, 30 January, 6 March, 27 April 1847; *Proceedings*, p. 1080.

service, the sheriffalty, increasingly became the object of bargain and sale, and this situation was constitutionally debilitating. Furthermore, the deficiencies of the courts and their members which had existed before the beginnings of the two-party system—cumbersomeness, disorderliness, inexpertness, and inattentiveness—persisted. In short, many believed it was time for change.

Despite fears that county government officials would tamper with the election returns to defeat the attempt for a call,[21] there is no evidence that they did so; even if they did, it was for naught because the proconvention forces overwhelmingly carried the question in August 1847, with 92,639 affirmative votes out of 136,945 cast. Having won the first round, the reformers were required to carry the question once more to the voters the following year. According to Ben Hardin, the officeholders, realizing that the voters would approve a convention, "pitched in, and swore they were in the hunt from the start . . . ; when they saw the convention was a beautiful trade wind, how they spread their sails . . . great God how they pitched in!"[22] The opposition having crumbled, the conventionists won the second round by an even greater margin.

Most of the candidates in the election for delegates supported revision of the county court system. Jefferson Evans, candidate for delegate from Greenup County, referred to the system as "a dead carcass." Sam Hanson, candidate from Clark County, described the courts as "unwieldy, . . . inefficient," and "totally unsuited to the correct and rapid dispatch of judicial business." Garrett Davis and George W. Williams of Bourbon County and Robert W. Scott of Franklin County, all candidates, also denounced the existing system. Even Samuel Shy, a candidate from Fayette

21 On 24 July 1847 the *Convention* urged the sheriffs of the various counties to do their duty and hold honest elections on the question of calling a convention. The newspaper feared that some sheriffs would refuse to do this.

22 *Commonwealth*, 21 September 1847; *Proceedings*, p. 1080.

County, who depicted the old order as "one of the best, wisest and cheapest systems known to the law," favored electing members of the county courts.[23] The elections produced a victory not only for the supporters of court reform but also for the Democratic party, which had been decidedly in the minority for most of its twenty-two-year history. In accordance with the Constitution, which was about to be abolished, the voters elected 100 delegates—52 Democrats and 48 Whigs.

Although slavery, legislative apportionment, and the method of selecting judges of the Court of Appeals were the subjects of most of the debates of the convention, the reform of the county court system played an important part in the proceedings. Many delegates believed that the defects of the system provided the *raison d'être* for the convention. George W. Kavanaugh, delegate from Anderson County, contended that "we, to-day, would not have been here forming a constitution, but for the universal dissatisfaction felt against our county courts," and many others seconded his remarks. Nevertheless, there was considerable division among the delegates concerning what changes were necessary. There was naturally a broad range of sentiment on the extent of failure in the county courts and the need for revision. Those who desired the most profound alteration saw the widest variety of faults. Larkin Proctor found the entire system "odious," the one thing that the people of Kentucky unanimously wanted "abolished," and Richard L. Mayes of Graves County contended that the courts had met "the unqualified condemnation of the country" and called for sweeping reforms.[24]

On the other hand, those seeking milder reforms generally saw only two basic defects in the old system: the manner of appointing magistrates and the lifetime term of

[23] *Commonwealth*, 20 March, 10 April 1849; *Yeoman*, 14 June 1849; *Observer and Reporter*, 7 April, 7 July 1849.

[24] *Proceedings*, pp. 696–99, 701, 704, 708, 710–11.

office. They denied that the local tribunals were more unpopular than other courts or departments of government.
John T. Rogers of Barren County accused some of his colleagues of attempting to make the "county court ... the
scapegoat for others' sins." Thomas W. Lisle of Green
County argued that "the complaint has not been greater
against the county courts than the court of appeals and
the circuit court," while James M. Nesbitt of Bath County believed that "the principal grievance the people have
labored under, is the manner in which the court is
constituted."[25]

Once the delegates got down to the business of reform,
one basic question emerged: who would constitute the
newly devised county courts—one or more judges, or the
justices of the peace? After rejecting a variety of proposals,
the reformers agreed upon a compromise: each county court
would consist of a presiding judge and two associate judges,
with the provision that the legislature might abolish the
office of associate judge and substitute for it the justices of
the peace who would sit on the court of claims. Virtually all
the delegates agreed that the judges and magistrates should
be elected, the latter by districts within each county.[26] The
Constitution as approved by the delegates also provided
that the "jurisdiction of the county court ... shall be the
same now vested in the county courts of this State." Yet
early in the meeting the drafters had done away with a
significant power of the county courts by eliminating the
privilege of appointing sheriffs, jailers, surveyors, coroners,
constables, clerks, and county attorneys, all of whom would
be elected under the new Constitution.[27]

25 Ibid., pp. 695, 703, 714–15.
26 Ibid., pp. 127, 437, 697–719. Early in the proceedings Squire Turner, a
delegate from Madison County, introduced a resolution requiring that all
judges of "inferior courts" be lawyers, but it was not considered again; it
was the only attempt at the convention to convert the county courts into
"lawyers' courts." Ibid., p. 25.
27 Ibid., pp. 111, 356, 363, 377, 391–92, 403, 413–17, 420–28.

The constitutional reformers had eliminated some but not all of the grievances which had attached themselves to the county court system. They had made the courts theoretically democratic and free of oligarchy. They had seemingly removed much unwieldiness by providing that not more than three judges instead of multitudes should execute most of the judicial business of a county. They had minimized, if not eliminated, the possibility of malapportionment. They had made it more difficult to sell county offices. Yet they had left untouched some glaring weaknesses in the structure of local government. They had not proscribed magistrates from the legislature; neither had they established separate probate courts nor required that county judges be lawyers. The prejudice of many delegates against a professional elite seems to have undercut efforts to create a tribunal specializing in wills and estates and to require technical expertise among all judges. However, the most serious obstacle to more complete reform appears to have been the assumption by the delegates that Kentuckians would be unwilling to tax themselves to secure better and more efficient county government.

Few delegates to the Convention of 1849 were acting justices of the peace, although substantial numbers were magistrates *emeritus*. Seven of the one hundred delegates at the convention were acting justices of the peace, and seventeen others had served as magistrates within the last twelve years. Four of these twenty-four participated in the debate on the county court system, and all but one voted in at least one of the ballots concerning this issue. James P. Hamilton of Larue County was the only acting magistrate to participate in the debate. While he admitted that the county court system was "a rotten concern," he nonetheless favored changing only the method of appointing its members and its own appointing power, while retaining the magistrates as its members. He argued that if the legislature increased their fees, they would perform adequately. He opposed a court composed of three judges, who, he contended, would "come in, like so many Julius Caesars, to tax the people whether they like it or not." After the delegates voted to reconsider the motion to establish a three-judge court, Hamilton moved unsuccessfully to allow the legislature complete discretion to determine "the number of judges, their duty and salary." [28]

Two of the three ex-magistrates who spoke during the debate also favored a stronger role for the justices of the peace on the county courts than that which was ultimately provided by the convention. David Meriwether, who had served on the Jefferson County Court, offered an amendment early in the discussion which would have established county courts of one presiding judge together with the county magistrates. Richard D. Gholson, formerly a member of the Ballard County Court, was more restrained in his position on the proper place of the magistrates in county government; he favored allowing the justices of the peace to "sit on questions of claims and roads" only. The final participant in the debates, James H. Garrard, formerly of the Clay County Court, strongly supported the three-judge plan. [29]

In seven significant ballots three of the acting magistrate delegates can be classified as generally opposed to strengthening the position of justices of the peace, two in favor, and two ambivalent. Of the seventeen ex-magistrates, nine generally supported the interests of the justices of the peace, seven generally opposed them, and one did not vote. In all, eleven generally supported the magistrate position, ten generally opposed it, two vacillated, and one did not vote. Thus magistrates and ex-magistrates did not vote as a bloc but tended to divide evenly on the question of the proper powers

28 *Proceedings*, p. 705.
29 Ibid., pp. 695, 706, 714.

and responsibilities of justices of the peace within county government.

Among the delegates as a whole the Whigs tended to favor more sweeping reform of the county court system than did the Democrats. In two principal ballots the Whigs voted thirty-seven to six in favor of the modified three-judge measure which was incorporated into the Constitution, while voting twenty-nine to eleven against a last-minute effort to provide for an all-magistrate court. Democrats were more narrowly divided, voting twenty-six to sixteen in favor of the modified three-judge measure and twenty-one to twenty against the all-magistrate court. Significantly, they furnished the bulk of the support for the latter scheme.[30]

By late December 1849 the delegates had finished the business of drafting and approving a new Constitution and had instructed the sheriffs to open the polls in early May to take the sentiments of the voters "in regard to adoption or rejection" of the document. It was not a foregone conclusion that the voters would approve the charter; many of the delegates feared that if it were submitted to a popular vote, the members of the old county courts and their allies would somehow convert what had been an overwhelming sentiment for reform into a victory for the *status quo*. John D. Taylor, delegate from Mason County, predicted that the county officialdom would enlist their "friends and relations, their sons and their sons-in-law, and sons-in-law in expectation, and their daughters too . . . against this constitution, not because it does not accord with popular sentiment, but because it strikes at the root of their monopoly." Others foresaw that the magistrates would ally with the emancipationists, who were distraught by the failure of the delegates to abolish slavery, and other dissidents to thwart the will of

[30] A list of the party affiliation of the delegates can be found in the Louisville *Daily Journal*, 13 September 1849. The votes are recorded in *Proceedings*, pp. 716, 718.

the convention. Some believed that the agents of county government would actually refuse to open the polls to obtain an expression of the popular feeling. Still others envisioned that if the voters ratified the Constitution, the magistrates and their allies would refuse to abandon their offices on the grounds that the old frame of government had somehow not been legally abolished.

Although many of the courthouse clique undoubtedly campaigned against the Constitution, there is no indication that they allied with the abolitionists or that they conducted an improper election. Most of the ostensible opponents did not directly defend the old county court system but rather wisely camouflaged their sentiments by reviving the crusade which had worked for them in 1838, namely the fight to preserve an independent judiciary. There were new lines of defense also. Chilton Allen, a leading politician from Clark County, interjected Know-Nothingism into his pleas in behalf of an independent judiciary and predicted that if the Constitution were ratified, Roman Catholic bishops would commence instructing hordes of immigrants, who were allegedly pouring into the state, on how to vote. A correspondent to the Lexington *Observer and Reporter,* one of the few who openly defended the county courts, attempted to evoke regional prejudice by characterizing the old as the "Virginia gentlemanly court of justices" and the new as "the yankee 'Picayune Butler' system of pay-justices." These degrading appeals were in vain, however, for in May the voters ratified the new Constitution, 71,653 votes to 20,302.[31]

In March 1851 the legislature, doubtless attentive to the frugality that had manifested itself at the constitutional convention, abolished the office of associate judge of the county court and provided that the justices of the peace

31 *Observer and Reporter,* 3 October 1849, 10 April 1850; *Daily Journal,* 16, 18, 31 January, 16 February 1850; *Commonwealth,* 28 May 1850.

should have a limited place on the local tribunal.[32] By law it was specified that the presence of a majority of magistrates was necessary for the court to levy taxes and to make major appropriations, including those for the poor, roads, buildings, and bridges. At the same session the legislators granted minor civil jurisdiction to the county judges, thereby somewhat diluting that of the justices of the peace, and allocated magisterial districts to the counties, providing for over three hundred fewer justices of the peace than had existed before constitutional reform.[33]

In May 1851 special elections were held to select county judges, justices of the peace, and other county officials. Although it is impossible to determine how many magistrates who served under the old county court system sought office under the new, the number who were elected to county judgeships and magistracies can be estimated. Election returns for eighty-seven counties indicate that in thirty-six of them candidates who had been acting justices of the peace at the termination of the old system were elected to county judgeships. In ten others candidates who had served as magistrates sometime between 1837 and 1850 but who had retired before the end of the old order were returned to judgeships. Thus in slightly over half of the eighty-seven counties magistrates under the old system were elected to positions of leadership under the new. On the other hand, a much smaller proportion of the newly elected justices of the peace had served as magistrates under the old system. Records for twenty-five of the state's one hundred counties indicate that slightly fewer than one-fourth of the newly elected justices of the peace had served as magistrates between 1837 and 1851.[34]

---

32 *Acts, 1850–1851*, chap. 419.

33 Ibid., chap. 39.

34 Slightly over 92 percent of these had been acting magistrates in 1851, while slightly less than 8 percent had retired before then. Furthermore, only

In summary, about one-fifth of the county executives acting under the old Constitution at the time of its demise
continued in office under the new, either as county judges or
as magistrates. A far greater proportion of county judges
than of newly elected justices of the peace had been magistrates under the former system. The reasons for this are
obvious. The magistracy was far less attractive under the
third Constitution than under the second. It had only a
limited place on the county court and was stripped of its
most appealing prerogative, the sheriff's office. Conversely,
the office of county judge was a position of unprecedented
power in local government.

On paper the constitutional reformers of 1849 had
wrought profound changes in local government. The county court was no longer oligarchical, but democratic. Executive power was no longer diffused among ten or twenty
magistrates but was concentrated in the office of a single
county judge. And although the magistrates continued to
have a place on the county court, their role was restricted
and their representation apportioned. Finally, the first
county elections held under the new Constitution had resulted in a major turnover in the ranks of the magistracy
and a substantial number of new leaders.

Yet it is questionable whether the reforms of 1849 altered the reality as well as the form of county government.
The recorded debates of Kentucky's fourth and most recent
constitutional convention, held in 1890 and 1891, indicate

16.6 percent of the magistrates in office (73 of 439) in 25 sample counties on
the eve of constitutional reform continued in office under the new Constitution. The names of newly elected county judges may be found in the *Commonwealth*, 20, 27 May, 3 June 1851. Names of magistrates may be found in
the appropriate county court order books. The counties in this sample were
Bath, Boone, Bourbon, Bullitt, Christian, Fayette, Fleming, Franklin, Fulton, Garrard, Grant, Harrison, Henderson, Hickman, Jessamine, Madison,
Mason, Nicholas, Oldham, Pendleton, Shelby, Todd, Trigg, Woodford, and
Washington.

that many deficiencies of the old county court system persisted under the new. Delegates complained that during the life of the Constitution of 1849 the legislature continually increased the numbers of magistrates in each county and thereby made the court of claims (increasingly referred to after the Civil War as the "fiscal court") unwieldy. They charged that although the Constitution of 1849 had made most of the county offices elective, the county judges still retained some forms of patronage, which they dispensed unfairly. They further argued that few of the county judges were lawyers, and thus their administration of justice, especially in probate and petty criminal matters, was inept and sometimes farcical. They also contended that because their duties under the Constitution of 1849 were so insignificant most of the justices of the peace were incompetent. Finally, at least one delegate implied that some county judges were under the thumb of railroad companies.[35] Despite these allegations of incompetence, inefficiency, and corruption, the constitutional reformers of 1890–1891 made only minor changes in the county court system. They limited the maximum number of magistrates to eight per county and made it possible for the legislature to authorize individual counties to adopt a commission-type fiscal court in lieu of one comprised of justices of the peace and the county judge.[36]

Not surprisingly, county government under the Constitution of 1891 was just as inadequate as that under the

[35] *Official Report of the Proceedings and Debates in the Convention . . . of . . . 1890 to Adopt, Amend or Change the Constitution of the State of Kentucky*, 4 vols. (Frankfort, Ky., 1890), 3:3574, 3576, 3581–83, 3597–98.

[36] Under the commission form of fiscal court, county voters elect three commissioners who, along with the county judge, constitute the court. By 1964 only 15 of Kentucky's 120 counties had adopted a commission form of fiscal court. Kenneth Vanlandingham, *The Constitution and Local Government*, Kentucky Legislative Research Commission Informational Bulletin no. 36 (Frankfort, Ky., 1964), p. 15.

Constitutions of 1792, 1799, or 1849. A commentator writing in 1938 submitted that the fiscal affairs of the county courts were steeped in secrecy, that tax assessment and collection were inefficient, and that the administration of justice was affected by "rampant politics." He further contended that only 20 of 120 county judges were lawyers and that many judges, as well as justices of the peace, lacked even a high school education.[37] These shortcomings, plus others affecting both state and local government, prompted the legislature to authorize three referendums between 1931 and 1960 to take the sense of the people on whether to convene a constitutional convention. In each instance the voters rejected a call.

Finally, in 1964, the legislature established a Constitution Revision Assembly to draft a new state Constitution. Included in the proposed charter drawn up by this assembly were provisions which profoundly altered the nature of county government. The drafters stripped the county judge and the justices of the peace of their judicial functions. Furthermore, they proposed that many officers of local government, including the county judge and the sheriff, not be of constitutional origin, thus making it possible for the legislature alone to abolish these positions or make them appointive. It also stipulated that the General Assembly, with voter approval, could consolidate counties. The legislature submitted the proposed Constitution to the voters in the November 1966 election.[38]

Fearing that their offices and very counties were in jeopardy, the officials of Kentucky's county government, including many county judges and magistrates, led the fight to

[37] Henry C. Pepper, "County Government in Kentucky," (typescript in King Library, ca. 1938). By 1964 only 14 of 120 county judges were lawyers. Louisville *Courier-Journal*, 28 May 1964.

[38] Louisville *Courier-Journal*, 18 February, 28 May, 5 July 1964, 29 December 1965; Lexington *Herald*, 4 December 1965.

defeat the proposed Constitution at the polls. The Kentucky Sheriffs Association sounded the cry in May 1966 when it branded the newly drafted charter as an attempt to destroy county government; later it implied that the goal of the reformers was a communist dictatorship. This chant was soon taken up by other organizations, such as the Kentucky Magistrates and Commissioners Association, and by count-less county officials. W. C. Flannery, judge of the Rowan County Court, in a letter to all his fellow county judges, depicted the new Constitution as an endeavor to establish a "police state," while the clerk of Jefferson County de-nounced the document as a bid to create "a monarchy in Frankfort." [39]

Unlike the courthouse cliques of 1850, the county of-ficials of 1966 were successful in their attempt to defeat the proposed Constitution. Kentuckians rejected the charter by a margin of more than three and a half to one. [40] Thus for all their democratic appearance, the county courts of mod-ern Kentucky retain many of the deficiencies of their coun-terparts before the Civil War, and these weaknesses are likely to prevail for many years to come. The old county court system may be dead, but its spirit lingers on.

[39] Louisville *Courier-Journal*, 15 May, 15, 28 June, 10 August, 13, 22 October 1966; Lexington *Herald*, 16 May 1966.

[40] Louisville *Courier-Journal*, 9 November 1966. James Hunt, legislative representative from Pike County, was most prophetic when he warned in March 1966 that "the courthouse gang is not going to let this [the Constitu-tion] pass unless we leave their names in it." Louisville *Courier-Journal*, 19 March 1966.

Conclusion

THE COUNTY COURTS affected the people of antebellum Kentucky more profoundly than any other governmental institution. The miller, the apprentice, the heir, the ferry operator, the tavern owner, the land speculator, the profligate, the vagrant, the poor, the taxpayer, the orphan, and the slave all dealt with the local tribunals. The business of the courts encompassed a series of legal specialties in combination with significant prerogatives of government and patronage.

Despite their great powers, the courts were not without countervailing institutions. The governor served as a check on their dispensation of county patronage. The legislature delegated and withdrew the courts' authority and on occasion established superseding agencies such as cities, incorporated towns, and turnpike companies. The Court of Appeals and the circuit courts, when duly petitioned, reviewed their judicial decisions.

The county courts did not usually seek to expand their constitutional niche by innovation as did their English counterparts throughout the eighteenth and early nineteenth centuries.[1] When a particular county court was uncertain of its powers or responsibilities, or when it had delayed or neglected to perform some function, it usually sought clarification or ratification from the General Assembly. Notwithstanding this constitutional timidity, there were occasions when courts assumed questionable powers without legislative confirmation, as in the case of some of their investments in enterprises of internal improvement; or when they acted in extralegal fashion, as in the case of their patronage nominations by means of rump sessions; or when they manifested outright defiance of higher constitutional authorities, as in the cases of the Franklin County Court's nullification of a Court of Appeals decree in 1845 or the Fayette County Court's nullification of a new road law in 1834; or when they engaged in illegal activities such as the sale of public office.

As in England, the justices of the peace of Kentucky, as the principal governors of the local constitution, may have been the "most influential class of men"[2] in the Commonwealth. Certainly they had the powers, positions, and prestige to be. They were the directors of what was in many ways the most pervasive portion of the state constitution. Most of them came from relatively high socioeconomic groups and were members of the political-military elite. Nevertheless, it is doubtful that they gave Kentucky, as it can be argued their counterparts gave Elizabethan England, "the best local government in the world."[3] One reason for this was their failure to be as self-sacrificing or as well-trained as their English predecessors. Most were not lawyers and neglected to educate themselves in the subtleties of their very specialized judicial business. Without the stimulus of salaries or fees for their services on the county courts, too many of them invited reform by their persistent inattention to the duties of the system. They sat too little, too late, or not at all; they failed to maintain consistency or decorum in the dispatch of business; and they eventually succumbed to their own brand of partisanship and venality —all of which contributed to their constitutional demise.

The collapse of the old county court system was also hastened by its commitment to oligarchy. County voters

[1] Sidney Webb Passfield and Beatrice Webb Passfield, *English Local Government: A Series . . . on the Growth and Structure of English Local Government*, 11 vols. (London, 1906), vol. 1, *The Parish and the County*, pp. 480–556.

[2] J. H. Gleason, *The Justices of the Peace of England, 1558–1640* (Oxford, 1969), p. 96.

[3] Ibid., p. 115.

and taxpayers had no express role in the selection of court members or in the formation of county policy. In most cases the courts filled their own vacancies without consulting their constituents, and too often the county courts formulated and executed policy without securing popular approval. This is not to say that democratic pressures were never effectively brought to bear on the county courts. Outraged citizens at times petitioned the legislature seeking statutory reversal of an unpopular policy, and from time to time members of a particular region or political party successfully petitioned the governor to ignore the recommendations of county courts on the dispensation of patronage. Courts themselves occasionally initiated the democratic process by authorizing precinct elections to obtain popular opinion on would-be magistrates. In other instances the legislature ordered county courts to consult the voters by means of referendums on such weighty issues as county subscriptions to turnpike or railroad stock, although at times the courts themselves voluntarily authorized such elections. Yet these constitutional and extraconstitutional devices were so infrequently used and so unreliable that the democracy practiced by the county courts was an exception to their generally aristocratic tendencies.

The failure of the legislature to deal meaningfully with the numerous shortcomings of the county courts also contributed to their downfall. Although attempts were made to reform the county court system by means of legislation, none was successful. It should be reiterated, however, that this was due not to a monolithic cabal of self-interested justices of the peace in the assembly but rather to a general tendency of legislators to ignore the grievances arising from the practices of county government.

Certainly the impact of the two-party system in Kentucky helped bring on the collapse of the county court system. It organized the factional bickering which had always plagued the courts, stressed more than ever politicking over performance, and accelerated the processes of geographical malapportionment. Above all, it frustrated scores of party leaders who, although they continually won at the polls, were often excluded from the ranks of the county oligarchy.

Just as clearly, one party did not monopolize the county courts of antebellum Kentucky. Both parties benefitted from their oligarchical nature, although the Democrats may well have gained the most from the constitutional provision which allowed the membership of the courts to perpetuate itself. It may well have been that many Jacksonians sought refuge in county magistracies as their ability to win elections to other offices diminished. We have seen that of five of twenty sample county courts dominated by parties not successful at the county polls, four were Democratic. So, too, Democrats were more numerous among the magistrates in the legislature than in the membership at large, a fact which might indicate that there were more Democrats in the county court system than in any other governmental institution of the state. Certainly Jacksonian zeal for reform of local government, which was never very great, receded in the wake of continuing Whig victories.

It is evident, too, that the death of the old county court system did not come as the result of an unprecedented outpouring of Jacksonian sentiment. The quest to reform the local tribunals was bipartisan. Indeed the caucus of seventy-six legislators, which in 1846 cited an ineffective county court system as a reason for a constitutional convention, was composed of almost equal numbers of Whigs and Democrats. The relative lack of Whig enthusiasm for general constitutional reform resulted not because of a commitment to the county court system but rather because many feared that a new charter would dilute the strength of the party by undoing its gerrymandering. When the convention met, most Whig delegates supported basic reform of the county court system, while many Democrats endorsed a weaker revision.

In the end the old county court system of Kentucky was struck down at the hands of reformers when its most obvious virtue, inexpensiveness, became outweighed by the burden of its many faults.

Governors of Kentucky

1792–1851

Isaac Shelby	1792–1796
James Garrard	1796–1804
Christopher Greenup	1804–1808
Charles Scott	1808–1812
Isaac Shelby	1812–1816
George Madison	1816
Gabriel Slaughter	1816–1820
John Adair	1820–1824
Joseph Desha	1824–1828
Thomas Metcalfe	1828–1832
John Breathitt	1832–1834
James T. Morehead	1834–1836
James Clark	1836–1839
Charles A. Wickliffe	1839–1840
Robert P. Letcher	1840–1844
William Owsley	1844–1848
John J. Crittenden	1848–1850
John L. Helm	1850–1851

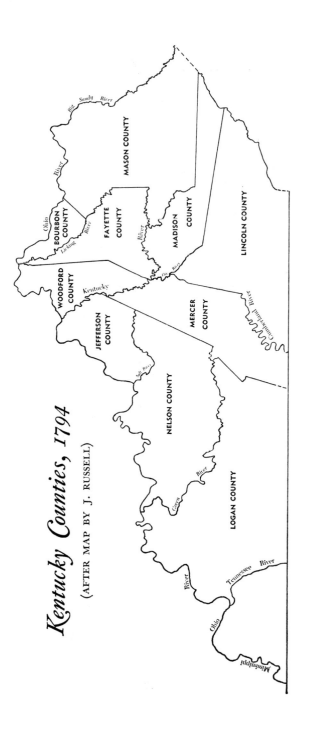

Kentucky Counties, 1794

(AFTER MAP BY J. RUSSELL)

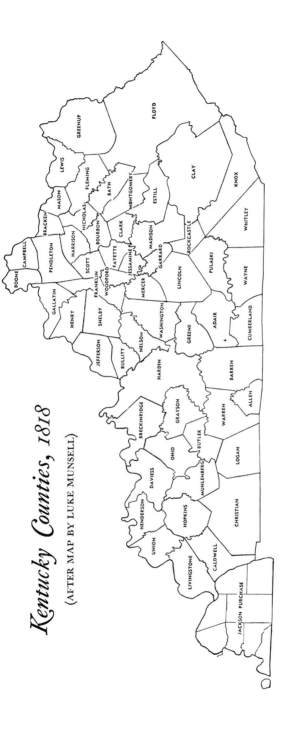

Kentucky Counties, 1818

(AFTER MAP BY LUKE MUNSELL)

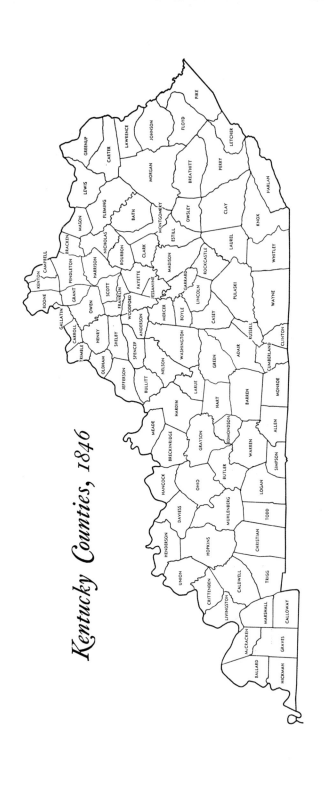

Kentucky Counties, 1846

An Essay on Authorities

AN INDISPENSABLE, though dated, guide for scholars studying any aspect of Kentucky history is J. Winston Coleman's *A Bibliography of Kentucky History* (Lexington, Ky.,
1949).

Government Documents

Published and unpublished governmental records were a
treasure trove of authorities for this study of the county courts
of Kentucky. Among the most significant of the unpublished
records are the Papers of the Governors of Kentucky, located
at the Kentucky State Historical Society in Frankfort and available on microfilm. Emma Guy Cromwell's *A Catalogue of the
Records, Documents, Papers . . . of the Governors of Kentucky,
1792–1926* (Frankfort, Ky., 1926) furnishes a generally reliable
description of the contents of this collection. The most useful
types of documents in the Papers are the journals and letterbooks of the governors, the registers of justices of the peace, lists
of justices of the peace for particular years, and letters, petitions,
recommendations, and other documents relating to justices of
the peace, sheriffs, and other county officers.

The order books of the county courts are also an invaluable
source. They provide an excellent summary of the business of
the courts and insights on such matters as attendance and intra-
court disputes. Not all the order books for all one hundred of
Kentucky's counties (to 1851) are extant, but most of those
which do exist have been microfilmed by the Church of Jesus
Christ of Latter Day Saints, and copies of this film are available
at the King Library, University of Kentucky. Those counties
whose order books were most useful for this study are Anderson, Bath, Boone, Bourbon, Boyle, Bracken, Bullitt, Caldwell,
Christian, Estill, Fayette, Fleming, Franklin, Fulton, Garrard,
Grant, Harrison, Henderson, Hickman, Jefferson, Jessamine,

Lincoln, Madison, Mason, Montgomery, Nicholas, Oldham, Pendleton, Scott, Shelby, Todd, Trigg, Washington, Whitley, and Woodford. Journals of a similar nature, the Record Books of the Town and City of Lexington, 1780–1836, are extremely helpful in establishing the constitutional and political relationship between the Fayette County Court and the town and city of Lexington. These books are located at the Lexington Municipal Building.

Both the state tax records, microfilm of which is located at the Kentucky State Historical Society, and the federal censuses, microfilm of which is located at the King Library, are useful in compiling collective biographies of the members of the county courts.

Finally, the judgments of the circuit courts provide some insights into the relationship of those tribunals to the county courts. Microfilm of some of these documents is located at the King Library.

Among the published government records which are most revealing with regard to the county courts are the *Acts of Kentucky, 1792–1851*; the *Journal of the House of Representatives, 1792–1851* and *Journal of the Senate, 1792–1851*; and the *Constitution of 1792, Constitution of 1799,* and *Constitution of 1849.* The *Acts* contain numerous statutes affecting the courts and county officers; the *Journals,* while not containing legislative debates, summarize well the business and some of the votes of the two houses, much of which was related to the courts and county officers; and the *Constitutions,* of course, embrace the fundamental provisions on county government.

One of the richest sources of information on the county courts is the *Report of the Debates and Proceedings of the Convention for the Revision of the Constitution of the State of Kentucky, 1849* (Frankfort, Ky., 1849). Delegates to that conclave were remarkably frank about the place of the courts in the constitution of the state. Their debates also tell much about the politics and deficiencies of the county court system. Likewise the *Official Report of the Proceedings and Debates in the Convention . . . of . . . 1890 to Adopt, Amend, or Change the Constitution of the State of Kentucky,* 4 vols. (Frankfort, Ky., 1890) reveals much about the weaknesses of the county courts under the Constitution of 1849.

The *Reports of the Decisions of the Court of Appeals, 1792–1851,* cited by the name of the reporter, are indispensable in establishing the relationship of the high tribunal to the county courts.

Unofficial Statutory Collections and Legal Digests

William Waller Hening's *The Statutes at Large: Being a Collection of All the Laws of Virginia, 1619–1792,* 13 vols. (New York and Philadelphia, 1819–1823) furnishes valuable information on the ancestry of the county courts of Kentucky. William Littell's *The Statute Law of Kentucky with Notes, Praelections, and Observations on the Public Acts . . . ,* 5 vols. (Frankfort, Ky., 1809–1819) fills gaps left by nonextant volumes of the *Acts* and offers incisive annotations on the county courts. The following statutory and judicial digests are also of great value: Littell and Jacob Swigert's *A Digest of the Statute Law of Kentucky: Being a Collection of All the Acts of the General Assembly . . . ,* 2 vols. (Frankfort, Ky., 1822); C. S. Morehead and Mason Brown's *A Digest of the Statute Laws of Kentucky of a Public and Permanent Nature . . . ,* 2 vols. (Frankfort, Ky., 1834); Preston S. Loughborough's *Kentucky Laws, Statutes, . . . of a Public and Permanent Nature passed since 1834* (Frankfort, Ky., 1842), and Benjamin Monroe and James Harlan's *Digest of Cases at Common Law and in Equity Decided by the Court of Appeals of Kentucky . . . 1792 to 1853,* 2 vols. (Frankfort, Ky., 1853).

Newspapers

The newspapers of antebellum Kentucky supply much knowledge about the county courts, especially concerning their politics and their shortcomings. Of special merit are those published in Lexington, namely the *Kentucky Gazette,* the *Kentucky Reporter,* the *Observer and Reporter,* and the *Intelligencer;* in Frankfort, namely the *Palladium,* the *Argus of Western Amer-*

ica, the *Commonwealth*, the *Kentucky Yeoman*, and the *Convention*; and in Louisville, namely the *Public Advertiser*, the *Daily Journal*, and the *Daily Focus*. Also of some use are the Paris *Western Citizen* and the Russellville *Weekly Messenger*. Certain issues of a contemporary newspaper, the Louisville *Courier-Journal*, tell much about recent attempts to alter the structure of county government in Kentucky. The Lexington *Herald*, another current publication, is of more limited value on this topic.

Manuscript Collections

Seemingly most of the politicians of Kentucky who were connected with the county court system confined their observations on local government to correspondence with the governor and thus their private papers yield very little information on the subject of this monograph. Some insights, however, can be found in the Papers of Joseph Hamilton Daveiss and the Papers of Orlando Brown, both located at the Filson Club in Louisville, and the Mason County Historical Papers, microfilm of which is located at the King Library.

Published Diaries, Correspondence, Travel Accounts, Histories, Memoirs, and Directories

Only a few sources in this group provide information on the county courts. Humphrey Marshall's *History of Kentucky*, 2 vols., 2d ed. (Frankfort, Ky., 1824) offers pungent comments on the alleged influence of the magistrates in the legislature. Providing biographical information on Fayette County magistrates are William Leavy's "Memoir of Lexington and Its Vicinity With Some Notice of Many Prominent Citizens and Its Institutions of Education and Religion," *Register, Kentucky State Historical Society* 40 (1941): 107–31, 253–67, 353–75; 41 (1942): 44–62, 107–37, 250–60, 310–46; 42 (1943): 26–53; *Lexington's First City Directory, 1806* (Lexington, Ky., 1953); *Lexington's Second City Directory, 1818* (Lexington, Ky., 1953); and Julius P. Bolivar Maccabe's *Directory of the City of Lexington, 1838*

(Lexington, Ky., 1838). Finally, G. Glenn Clift's *The "Corn Stalk" Militia of Kentucky, 1792–1811* (Frankfort, Ky., 1957) furnishes significant data on the early Kentucky militia.

Monographs, Articles, and Dissertations

In addition to the works cited in the Preface, there are some useful studies not directly related to county government. Richard P. McCormick's *The Second American Party System: Party Formation in the Jacksonian Era* (Chapel Hill, N.C., 1966) and Leonard P. Curry's "Election Year: Kentucky, 1828," *Register, Kentucky State Historical Society* 55 (July 1957): 196–212, deal with antebellum Kentucky politics. Perry Miller's *The Life of the Mind in America: From Revolution to the Civil War* (New York, 1965) puts Kentucky's fight to preserve an independent judiciary into proper historical focus. Jasper B. Shannon and Ruth McQuown's *Presidential Politics in Kentucky, 1824–1948* (Lexington, Ky., 1950) and Shannon, McQuown, and Frank Mathias's "Gubernatorial Politics in Kentucky, 1820–1851" (manuscript in possession of authors) offer useful election statistics on a county-by-county basis. Mathias's "The Turbulent Years of Kentucky Politics, 1820–1850" (Ph.D. diss., University of Kentucky, 1966) furnishes information on the issues of state politics in antebellum Kentucky. Lewis and Richard H. Collins's *History of Kentucky*, 2 vols. (Covington, Ky., 1874) contains lists of legislators supplementing those in the legislative journals, not all of which are extant. Carl R. Field's "The Making of Kentucky's Third Constitution" (Ph.D. diss., University of Kentucky, 1951) provides some background material on the Constitutional Convention of 1849. Useful accounts of the twentieth-century county courts are Kenneth Vanlandingham's *The Constitution and Local Government*, Kentucky Legislative Research Commission Informational Bulletin no. 36 (Frankfort, Ky., 1964) and Henry C. Pepper's "County Government in Kentucky" (typescript in King Library, ca. 1938).

Index